Bill and Kim Wahl are two of the most effective and authentic leaders we've ever met. They've combined their wit, wisdom and Biblical insights to craft a modern masterpiece in their new book, *The Complaining Cure*. We love this book, and we genuinely believe this book has the potential to change your life, because it will help you change your mindset. In a world of negativity and darkness, we are called to be the light. This book crafts a powerful and practical plan to help you let go of the baggage of negativity and embrace the freedom, joy and peace that comes with God's plan.

Dave and Ashley Willis,
Authors, Speakers, and Podcasters for MarriageToday.

There is a cure for grumbling and complaining! Kim and Bill Wahl's book *The Complaining Cure: How to Quit Grumbling, Stop Criticizing and Find Abundant Joy*, provides not just sound biblical teaching on the subject, but transformational testimony from their own journey to joy in the midst of life's challenges. By providing "The Complaining Challenge" workbook as part of the book, the reader is encouraged to join the Wahls' journey to abundant joy. Contained in this book is truth that will change your life!

Faith Blatchford, Author/Speaker
Faithblatchford.com

What if just seven days from now you would be happier with everything in your life? In *The Complaining Cure* Bill and Kim give you the Spirit-inspired keys to controlling your tongue and, in so doing, reveal the biblical path to true joy and contentment. Studied alone or used in a group, you'll find a simple, seven-day approach to taming your tongue and changing your life forever.

Darren Schalk, Editor, One Accord Resources,
Author, Dear God, We Need to Talk, *Charisma House*

Bill and Kim Wahl's resolve and faith have inspired me to look for good in every situation. I have personally watched them handle adversity, and I have seen them weather storms few people could withstand. Through it all, they have confidently stood on the words of the Bible and have seen God do amazing things in their lives and ministry. If you have been through the fire, or if you are facing challenges that seem to be beyond your control, then this book is for you. As you go through this book, you will discover how positive words release God's power in your life. Read this book. Put these words into practice and your life will be better.

Dr. Marty Baker, Founder and Lead Pastor,
Stevens Creek Church/Founder, SecureGive

I have personally watched Bill and Kim live out the message of this book. They are not just authors, but real-life examples of the way God can use life when you decide to speak honor, faith, and encouragement, instead of criticism and negativity. When you finish this book, I believe your world will be different because your words will be different.

Jason Isaacs, Pastor at Hope City Church,
Author of Toxic Soul

The Complaining
CURE

The Complaining
CURE

HOW TO QUIT GRUMBLING,
STOP CRITICIZING,
AND FIND ABUNDANT JOY

BILL AND KIM WAHL

RIVER PUBLISHING

DEDICATION

We dedicate this book to Kim's dad, Albert Terrell Fike, Jr. (1946–2018). We can't remember hearing him say a judgmental or critical word about anyone. We never had "roasted pastor" for Sunday dinner. We never heard negative comments about the church, family, friends, neighbors, or coworkers. We always saw him choose to see the good, assume the best, and make allowances for faults. He lived out 1 Corinthians 13:7: "[Love] never stops believing the best for others" (TPT). May we follow in his footsteps and leave a legacy of love and kindness.

Do everything without complaining and arguing...

PHILIPPIANS 2:14

CONTENTS

CONTENTS

TESTIMONIALS

We promise you; this works. We are living witnesses to the needfulness and importance of this topic. We can also testify to the faithfulness of Father God and the powerful work of Holy Spirit in our lives to help us recover and heal from this sin and its damaging effects. But don't just take our word for it. Listen to these testimonies as well:

I enjoyed participating in the Challenge. It made me aware of how often complaining finds its way into my daily conversations. We often become deaf to what God and other people hear flow from our lips, and the Challenge opened my ears to what I was actually saying.

Dennis Bean – Charlotte, North Carolina

Engaging in the Challenge was a brilliant experience. So often we aren't aware of the words falling from our lips, right out of the hidden recesses of our heart. The Challenge brought heightened awareness to my every day words and more importantly my everyday thoughts, which allowed me to take those thoughts captive and lay them at the feet of Jesus. The result was greater levels of joy and connectivity with Jesus. Life changed!

Julie Gutierrez – Pleasant View, Utah

The Challenge has proven to be both timely and successful in my life. I was in a prolonged business relationship where continual opportunities arose for me to be greatly offended and discouraged. In times past, I allowed myself to complain, felt justified in doing it, but it never solved anything. As I looked to Holy Spirit for help, strength, and wisdom, He continually ministered to me and reminded me of the skills we learned in the Challenge. Not complaining didn't change anything around me, but greatly changed things in me. I do believe choosing not to complain enhanced my ability to hear Holy Spirit more clearly and quickly in order to navigate day by day throughout that relationship.

Tom Zawierucha – Wales, Michigan

I think if we are honest, most of us probably complain about something. When I did the Challenge, I was recovering from major surgery. I would wake up early and do the Challenge's devotion for the day before my feet hit the floor. I think starting the day focusing on the Challenge to not complain contributed to how my day went. Being aware of my complaints, catching myself before I began to complain, and focusing on choosing different words can really make a difference.

Amanda Downey – McKinney, Texas

Complaining and criticizing clearly blocks our relationship with Him and others. Through the Challenge, Holy Spirit opened my eyes and ears to see and hear more clearly.

Wayne Walker – Marine City, Michigan

I'm so grateful for the Challenge. Bill and Kim's insights brought daily conviction, and I was made aware by Holy Spirit how often my mouth ran away with me. I'm thankful because it encouraged me to come up higher. As a result, I experienced more joy in me, closer communion with family, and less anxiety and frustration. I am always ready for more of the Challenge.

Renée Rodriguez – Yuma, Arizona

I'm a fairly positive person. I try to stay positive and I typically do. So when I agreed to focus on my level of complaints for the Challenge, I thought I wouldn't have many. But when I focused on my attitude, I realized I complain more than I originally thought.

Margret Vanlderstine – Prince Edward Island, Ontario, Canada

What I first realized when going through the Challenge was how much I complained and that I was going to be able to stop only with the help of Holy Spirit. Because there is life and death in the tongue, I began to realize I am able to speak myself into having a good day or a bad day— despite the circumstances. The most important thing I learned is that complaining is the absence of thankfulness.

Tanja Lunney – Glenmora, Louisiana

The Challenge totally changed the way I spew my words on people and social media. Going through the Challenge led me to my biggest discovery: I had huge trust issues. Changing the way I think allowed His love to fill me to overflowing and helped me get unstuck so I could trust Jesus and people. Changing the way I talk allowed me to shine brighter and show others Jesus inside me. Do I get it right 100 percent of the time? Absolutely not. But I am one thousand times better than before the Challenge.

Martha Richardson – Madison, South Dakota

Well, I really didn't think about how much I complained. But as I got into the Challenge, the conviction hit me. I knew complaining wasn't good for me, but I had become complacent. This seven-day experience opened my eyes and helped me change. While I am still a work in progress, I am now aware and can hear His gentle reminders to let His mind be in me. This is my continual challenge.

Colleen Nieman – Oscoda, Michigan

The Challenge showed me how much I complain about people. It was during the Challenge that Holy Spirit showed me how to love people and want to serve them as a form of worship. Through many steps of learning to follow and simply obey, I've become more and more reliant on the Lord's voice to guide my every step. I'll serve people as a form of worship. There is no other way to live!

Trista Johns – Texas

Here are a few of my take-aways from the Challenge experience:
- Stop saying things that are mean-spirited.

- To even think negatively is a foothold for the enemy.

- I need to lift people up and not just be nice on the surface.

- Thinking complaining thoughts, or always looking for the "catch," is actually complaining.

- I realized when I said to my husband, "You should have done it this way, or done that instead," it was actually a back-door complaint.

I began to realize that we cannot change our thoughts by ourselves, and it's not an overnight process. We have to recognize the negative, stop it mid-sentence, then pray for the ability to see the good.

If we are trying to be like Jesus, we need His joy. People know we are Christians by our love that comes from the joy we have, not our complaints. I use the Bible verse that says, "Whatever is noble or good . . . think on these things," to help me change my thinking, and it's still in process. The joy of the Lord is my strength, and His joy is not mean and does not complain.

Dena Long – Capac, Michigan

ACKNOWLEDGMENTS

We'd first and foremost like to thank Jesus for asking us to partner with Him in this adventure. We are forever grateful that He would not only expose this issue in our lives and lead us to freedom but would also allow us to be the poster children for His message. He is amazing, and we are undone.

I (Kim) would like to thank my Rooted Group (women's discipleship group) for having open, honest, and vulnerable discussion with me about this topic. This group was the hothouse that gave this topic roots in my life and opened the door for this to unfold. Tammy Forbes, Ellen Goulette, Lydia Bricker, Lesa Bricker, Bev Lasky, Tara Fibranz, Judy LaGore, and Sue Armstrong, I loved every minute of our time together and appreciate the inspiration and encouragement you offered. Lydia, I am forever grateful you shared with us the strategy you and Ethan employ to defeat a critical spirit.

We'd also like to thank Tammy Forbes, Ellen Goulette, Rodney Bricker, and our son-in-law Scott Smith for being beta readers. Your encouragement, support, proofing, and insight was priceless, and we could not have done this without you. Thank you for cheering us on!

A big thank-you to Penny Ledezma and Sherry Susalla for the hours of prayer support during the months we worked on this project. Even though you had no idea what you were praying about, you were faithful to pray for us, and we are extremely grateful.

Much thanks to Rod and Lesa Bricker who gave us a place to hunker down and write in isolation. This was an incredible blessing!

ACKNOWLEDGMENTS

Our deepest love and appreciation to our family, The River Church in Fort Gratiot, Michigan, who loved, supported, encouraged, and prayed for us. You are a treasure, and we are honored to run with you.

Finally, we thank our friend Mary Conlan who first suggested writing a book and whose confidence encouraged us to try.

INTRODUCTION

Thank you for purchasing this book and stepping into this adventure with us. We call this an adventure because it has been an incredible journey for us. Holy Spirit has invited us into greater levels of joy and freedom by allowing us to partner with Him to remove the toxicity of complaining and criticism from our lives. Our desire is to share with you our discoveries that have proven to be a cure for a complaining and critical spirit. As we have partnered with Holy Spirit, we have indeed found greater joy.

We want to begin by letting you know that we are not pros at not complaining. In fact, the opposite is true; we've been certified Level 3 Complainers at times. A lot of the time. We've spent more than our fair share of time grumbling, whining, and criticizing. We've gone through seasons where that's all we would say. If you know us, we are certain you've heard us complain and criticize people, places, things, and ideas. We may have said critical things to you. And for that, we humbly apologize. We are truly sorry and ask you to forgive us.

So, we are not writing this book from an expert's perspective, or as one who has conquered complaining totally. We are writing it from the perspective of one who is continually learning as Holy Spirit reveals pockets of complaining and criticism in our lives. It is an on-going journey. It is a process. We continue to learn, grow, and develop in this area.

In all honesty, we stumbled upon this as God was doing some weeding in our lives. We never set out to write a book on this topic. We didn't plan on starting a movement. It just evolved, with one thing leading to another as Jesus took us on a personal journey.

In 2017, I (Kim) was leading a women's discipleship group when Holy Spirit dropped a topic for discussion in my heart: complaining. I didn't do a lot of prep or study before broaching the subject, but just took the one verse He gave me, Philippians 2:14, and started a conversation. As we talked, Holy Spirit began to unearth junk in all of us. For months we discussed complaining and all its various forms as Holy Spirit gave us revelation and brought conviction. It was powerful, sobering, painful, and liberating all at the same time.

It was during one of our many conversations that one of the girls mentioned that she and her husband would do a "complaining fast" when they found themselves in a negative season. That's when Holy Spirit zinged my heart. I promptly issued a challenge to abstain from complaining for seven days. They all accepted. Every morning, I sent a text with a mini-devotional and some Scripture to meditate on. At the end of the week, we were alive with awareness. We had been convicted, liberated, and empowered. We also knew this was just the surface. There was more to unearth, as this was a bigger problem than any of us had realized.

That's when Holy Spirit highlighted a series Bill and I had planned for November of that year entitled "Me and My Big Mouth." As Bill and I prepared, we felt Holy Spirit wanted me to speak on complaining during my week of this series and issue the same challenge to abstain from any form of complaining to our entire congregation. We held it the week before Thanksgiving; perfect timing to establish gratitude and thankfulness in our hearts.

It was a great week! God did some incredible things in us and our church family as we journeyed through this challenge together. Through the daily devotionals and live videos, we were connecting with truth. We heard incredible testimonies at the end of the week. Most said the Challenge was a giant *"aha!* moment," as Holy Spirit revealed hidden areas of negativity in their lives and helped them understand why they were prone to complaining. Some discovered the reason why they lived in discontentment and were never satisfied. Others said it helped them connect to the reasons why they struggled with ingratitude and had a lack of thankfulness. Many completed the week feeling liberated and energized as they felt the weight of negativity fall off them. Most said they felt empowered. We counted this corporate event as a great success!

While our congregation certainly learned, grew, and benefited from all the conversations and revelations, little did we know that God orchestrated the months of dialogue and the two rounds of challenges just for us.

On December 4, 2017, two weeks after the completion of the second Challenge, we discovered that the parsonage we'd been living in for a little over four years was contaminated with toxic levels of mold and formaldehyde. Months of illness and unexplainable symptoms for Bill, and a four-year battle with chronic respiratory, bronchial, and sinus infections (among a long list of other issues) for me, along with respiratory struggles for our son, Stefan, suddenly began to make sense.

Upon the advice of professionals, we immediately moved out and waited to hear if we would be able to keep our possessions. We stayed in a hotel for a few days and then accepted the gracious offer of our wonderful friends, Gary and Vickie Brown, to stay in an apartment in their warehouse. Just two weeks before Christmas we learned almost everything we owned had to be discarded. Thrown away. Trashed.

Insurance didn't cover anything. The policies in place had no provision for mold. It was a total loss.

We were stunned. It all happened so fast. Within a week we went from living in a nice home full of nice things—completely decorated for Christmas, too!—to being homeless with very little. And that very little had to go through a stringent decontamination process. Items that could be saved had to be washed in the high temperatures of a commercial dishwasher, or hand washed with bleach, getting into the nooks and crannies of each piece. Any clothing we wanted to keep had to be dry cleaned. So it would be a while before we had more than just a bag of necessary items.

The plethora of emotions that rolled through us were overwhelming. The grief of losing almost everything. The pain of throwing away items that could not be replaced. The shame of owning so much. Owning too much. The relief that a few things here and there could be kept. The deep appreciation of our church family who helped us salvage what could be kept. Thankfulness for having an answer to our ongoing health problems.

Uncertainty for the future. Feeling unprepared and caught off guard. And all of that during the height of the Christmas season.

That's when we realized this journey through Philippians 2:14 had been the active goodness of God in our lives. He had been preparing us for months for this leg of the journey, filling our souls with powerful truth and revelation, and packing our bags with tools and resources to equip us to successfully navigate through this adventure. If God had not prepared our hearts in advance, this trial would have smothered us as it overwhelmed our senses with a barrage of negative thoughts and emotions. Negative words would have eaten us alive as we complained about losing almost everything, being homeless, and feeling uncertain. We would never have been able to find our way out of the hole that complaining would have put us in. But in His goodness, God had set us up for success! We just love that about Him!

So we knew we could not complain about this unexpected turn of events. We knew we could not grumble, gripe, protest, fuss, whine, moan, play the victim, or ask why. In the months prior to this, as we had talked about this subject, we had learned too much. We knew this would be the key to help us not just survive this experience but to thrive during it. This would be the key to connecting to the heart of our Father in a time when we needed it most.

We also knew there was an entire church family watching us navigate through this experience. Would we live what we teach when it really mattered? Would we do what we had encouraged them to do? Would we do what we said was not only possible but necessary? Would we demonstrate truth in a tangible way, so they could see God's Word and His promises in action? Would we prove God to be true?

Yes. There could be no other answer. We had to let the work done in our hearts be demonstrated in our lives. Even when no one was watching or listening. James 1:22 became very real to us: "But don't just listen to God's word. You must do what it says. Otherwise, you are only fooling yourselves." We knew we had to put into action all that we had learned; otherwise we'd fall into self-deception. Were we tempted at times to complain? Yes. Absolutely. There were times of weariness, fatigue, and disappointment that gave us opportunity to whine or be angry.

As we made trip after trip to the dumpster with possessions that looked perfectly fine, we felt moments of anger. As we were displaced during the Christmas season and wondered where we would spend Christmas Eve and Christmas Day with our family, we felt disappointment. Faced with so many decisions to make, we felt weary. House shopping during the Christmas season left us frustrated. As the emotional turmoil drained us, we felt fatigued. And in it all, we felt urges— strong urges—to complain.

We hesitated to put too much detail of our journey in this book because we certainly don't want anyone to perceive it as complaining. However, we want to be honest about this journey. We don't want you to think this was easy or simple. We don't want to mislead anyone into thinking this was effortless. It was a struggle. The first several months after we moved from the parsonage, it felt like we walked around in a fog. Not only did we continue to feel physically sick, we felt emotionally overwhelmed and exhausted. Our thinking processes had been affected by the mold, the formaldehyde, and the emotional overload. For quite some time we had struggled with difficulty concentrating, and now with the additional stress it was even more difficult. It was hard to remember things. We struggled with decision fatigue. It was difficult to process information. Our minds ran a million miles a minute, and yet felt sluggish at the same time. Our daughter Danielle and son-in-law Dylan had a baby shower just days after we moved into the new house. The entire day was a blur; we barely remember the event. She delivered our second grandson in February, and we felt like we were only half present for this monumental occasion.

Bill struggled with incessant dizziness. This began in March 2017 and did not improve when we moved from the house. There were days he could not drive at all. There were days he could drive short distances. There were days he started off driving, but by the end of the day could not drive home.

We felt disjointed and disconnected from life as we struggled to put everything back together and regain our balance, as we continued to work, lead, and teach at The River. The year 2018 was an uphill battle, and some days we felt like we were losing. There were days fear gripped our hearts and we felt panic. There were days we wondered if this would be our new norm. And some days, we just held each other as we cried.

But despite the struggle, we remained committed to living free from complaining. We held each other accountable and reminded each other of the prep work we'd just gone through. We leaned on Holy Spirit for strength and wisdom. We processed our emotions with Jesus and each other and chose to be thankful and grateful instead.

In the end, while the Blight of '17 (our code name for this experience) was one of the most difficult, trying, and stressful things we've ever been through, it was also one of the most wonderful and rewarding experiences we've ever been through. Instead of complaining our way through this season of adversity, we were prepared to be thankful and grateful. It was not easy. But it was so worth it. And that made all the difference. It changed the outcome. It changed us.

We share this story with you to let you know, we have lived this. We're not writing about theories of unproven theology. We have done it. Not just the Seven-Day Challenge we present within these pages, but we've lived it in real life where the rubber meets the road. And we testify to you, it's real and it works. There is a cure. Again, it was not always easy. It's still not always easy. But it is still always worth it. And it's way better than the complaining and criticizing we were so very familiar with.

Even though we are experienced in this, we are not experts, and we are not finished. We are continuing to grow in this area and develop a thankful heart as we purpose to stop complaining and quit criticizing. At the time of this writing, Bill is still struggling with health issues stemming from mold and formaldehyde toxicity that have yet to be fully resolved. He continues to experience some form of dizziness. And there are days we just want to scream complaints in frustration and disappointment as we adjust to the myriad of changes we've had to make in our lives or handle the setbacks we experience. However, Holy Spirit continues to remind us to stop complaining and choose surrender. Even though it's been a long journey, this perspective is enabling us to see the beauty of the journey and find countless treasures along the way. And it's teaching us a better way of life.

We hope you'll find this lesson as powerful and impactful as we did. We also hope you'll connect with tools to help you discover a greater freedom and navigate through your next trial—whatever it may be—with success.

Here's to discovering the cure to complaining.

Part**One**

The Science of
Complaining

1

BRACE FOR IMPACT

Before we launch into the Challenge, we want to spend a little time laying some ground work. We believe that if you understand the spiritual, mental, and physical implications of words, you will be more likely to fully engage in the Challenge and experience life-altering change.

We realize this is not a new subject. We know dozens upon dozens of wonderful books have been written about the importance and significance of words, and more than likely you've read at least one of them. But we think it's important to bring up this subject again because it appears the Body of Christ is still struggling with this issue. We don't think we can say it any better, but we think repetition is the key for breakthrough. Zig Ziglar said it this way: "Repetition is the mother of learning, the father of action, which makes it the architect of accomplishment."[1] We often need to hear something repeatedly before it clicks with us and enables us to shift into change. So if you've heard this before, stick with us because you might need to hear it again.

Words have an impact that reverberates within the soul. They make this type of impact because they have a creative force behind them. We know this because we have been made in the image of God. In Genesis 1:26–27, we read: "Then God said, 'Let us make human beings in our image, to be like us. They will reign over the fish in the sea, the birds in the sky, the livestock, all the wild animals on the earth, and the small animals that scurry along the ground.' So God created human beings in his own image. In the image of God he created them; male and female he created them."

God made humans in His image. The word "image" in this passage is the Hebrew word *tselem*, and the word "like" is the Hebrew word *demuth*. Both of these words are also used in Genesis 5:3: "When Adam was 130 years old, he became the father of a son who was just *like* him—in his very *image*. He named his son Seth" (emphasis added). While Seth was not Adam— he was not a clone or a duplicate identical to Adam—Seth was like Adam. He bore a strong resemblance to Adam and was similar, comparable to, and matched Adam in many ways. Seth could naturally do some of the things Adam could do because he was hardwired that way. Seth could do other things like Adam because Adam taught him how to do those things the same way he did them.

What does this mean to us? While we are *not* God—not a clone or a duplicate identical to God—we do bear a resemblance to Him and are similar in many ways. We can do some of the things God does because He hardwired us to be like Him. We can do other things like God because He teaches us how to do them the way He does them.

With that in mind, let's look at some of the things God does that we also do. God thinks. God feels. God sees. God hears. We do all of those things naturally because He hardwired us to do them. The wonder of this is that He teaches us how to think, feel, see, and hear the way He does.

God also speaks. His words have a creative force, forming everything we see and know. He speaks, and things happen. Look at these examples:

- Genesis 1:3—"Then God said, 'Let there be light,' and there was light."

- Psalm 33:6—"The LORD merely spoke, and the heavens were created. He breathed the word, and all the stars were born."

- Psalm 33:9—"For when he spoke, the world began! It appeared at his command."

- Psalm 148:5—"Let every created thing give praise to the LORD, for he issued his command, and they came into being."

- Hebrews 11:3—"By faith we understand that the entire universe was formed at God's command, that what we now see did not come from anything that can be seen."

God spoke, and an impact was made. Something happened. Something changed. Something was produced. Like God, we speak. Though we cannot speak something into existence from nothing, we do create with our words. We make an impact with our words. Our words bring change. Things are produced from our words. Good or bad, something happens when we speak. Look at these examples:

- Proverbs 18:21 (AMP)—"Death and life are in the power of the tongue, And those who love it and indulge it will eat its fruit and bear the consequences of their words."

The tongue has the power to produce. Our words either produce death or produce life.

- Proverbs 13:3—"Those who control their tongue will have a long life; opening your mouth can ruin everything."

Our words either bring longevity or put an end to things by ruining it.

- Proverbs 18:7–8—"The mouths of fools are their ruin; they trap themselves with their lips. Rumors are dainty morsels that sink deep into one's heart."

Our words can produce destruction and create a trap and have the ability to lodge within the heart.

- Proverbs 11:9—"With their words, the godless destroy their friends, but knowledge will rescue the righteous."

Our words either destroy people or rescue people.

- Proverbs 15:1—"A gentle answer deflects anger, but harsh words make tempers flare."

Our words produce calm or create a firestorm.

- Proverbs 15:4 (AMP)—"A soothing tongue [speaking words that build up and encourage] is a tree of life, But a perverse tongue [speaking words that overwhelm and depress] crushes the spirit."

Our words build people or crush them.

We're going to stop there, but if you'd like to see more evidence on the creative power of words, check out these verses. It's certainly not an exhaustive list, but it will definitely give you more insight into the power of words.

• Proverbs 12:6	• Proverbs 21:23
• Proverbs 12:13–14	• Proverbs 26:20–22
• Proverbs 12:18–19	• Matthew 15:11
• Proverbs 18:6–8	• 1 Peter 3:10–11

As you can see, the Bible has a lot to say about words and the importance of choosing ones that line up with truth. The Bible places this tremendous emphasis on words because they significantly impact our lives and the lives of others, whether positively or negatively. Our words are not just little puffs of air that slip through our lips and evaporate into nothingness. They are more like puffs of dynamite with a creative force behind them.

Each of these verses makes it clear that our words are producing something. If we could see into the spirit realm, we'd see that every word we say has a creative force behind it that creates pathways for our future. Our intangible words are building something very tangible. Something concrete. They either create

> *Our words are not just little puffs of air that slip through our lips and evaporate into nothingness. They are more like puffs of dynamite with a creative force behind them.*

pathways of longevity, peace, blessing, and life, or they are building roads that lead to entrapment, chaos, ruin, and death. They create worlds of serenity or drama. Our words lay a foundation for things to come. And, to some degree, our words are shaping our future. Words are incredibly powerful!

The problem is, we have failed to understand the tremendous power of words. We have underestimated the significance of these wisps of breath that breeze over our vocal cords. Sure, we know they can create a scene or hurt feelings. We may have even felt the shock of their sting. We also know words can warm our heart, boost our courage, or energize us, but we honestly have not grasped the continuing effects of words or the deep, lasting impact they make. Because words are intangible and seem to evaporate into nothingness, we have failed to realize those words have a seismic, long-term impact, for either good or bad, on us personally and those around us.

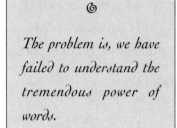

The problem is, we have failed to understand the tremendous power of words.

I (Bill) remember when I was in my early twenties and starting a career in restaurant management. I was newly saved, newly married, and emerging from a dark alcohol and drug addiction. I had a lot of baggage and immaturity, which made my intense personality a handful. I had spent six months in Tupelo, Mississippi, training in the management program for a large southern cafeteria-style restaurant, and was being transferred to Jackson, Tennessee, upon completion. Nervous, anxious, and wanting (needing) to succeed so badly, I met my new boss, Tom Green. I cannot begin to tell you the impact this man had on my life. His words were like a balm to my wounded soul. He was kind, firm but gentle, and patient with me. He never used his words to demean or belittle me. He constantly encouraged, even as he instructed and corrected. I had the honor and privilege of working with Mr. Green for five years, and during that time, his kind, supportive, and encouraging words changed the trajectory of my life. His words had a deep and lasting impact on me that I feel to this day.

THE POWER OF THE TONGUE

The reality is, words echo through eternity and have a lasting impression and enduring repercussions. Holy Spirit said it like this:

> And so the tongue is a small part of the body yet it carries great power! Just think of how a small flame can set a huge forest ablaze. And the tongue is a fire! It can be compared to the sum total of wickedness and is the most dangerous part of our human body. It corrupts the entire body and is a hellish flame! It releases a fire that can burn throughout the course of human existence. (James 3:5–6, TPT)

Holy Spirit is showing us that in relation to the small size of the tongue, the effects of it are disproportionately impactful. While the tongue is extremely small in proportion to the rest of the body, it has greater influence than any other part of the body. *The Message* paraphrases it like this:

> A word out of your mouth may seem of no account, but it can accomplish nearly anything—or destroy it! It only takes a spark, remember, to set off a forest fire. A careless or wrongly placed word out of your mouth can do that. By our speech we can ruin the world, turn harmony to chaos, throw mud on a reputation, send the whole world up in smoke and go up in smoke with it, smoke right from the pit of hell.

In this passage, Holy Spirit uses the example of a forest fire. Let's think about that for a moment. It takes only a small, tiny spark to set an entire forest aflame. Whether it was set intentionally, carelessly, or innocently, the effects are all the same. Once it's been set ablaze, it immediately begins to cause damage. Even though it can be halted and extinguished, the damage caused by that initial tiny spark is significant, impacting more than just trees.

For example, did you know that severely burned soil can become water-repellent? It's a phenomenon called *hydrophobicity*. The scorching of the fire prevents the soil from absorbing water. Without the ability to hold on to water, new life has difficulty growing. So instead of water being a benefit, it becomes a hindrance, eroding away topsoil. The runoff of ash and sediment from the topsoil often pollutes the rivers and streams nearby, becoming toxic to fish and other life. It has the potential to contaminate other wildlife nearby. Depending upon the severity of the fire, the length of time it burned, and how slowly it burned, it could take a decade or more for a forest to recover. Years after a fire has been extinguished, you see evidence of its rampage. You can see the charred remains and often smell the singed odor that hangs in the air.

We're so thankful Holy Spirit used the imagery of a fire, because it paints a powerful picture of the effect of words. Words can be the spark that sets a fire within our souls (our mind, will, and emotions), and within the souls of others. Words spoken innocently, carelessly, or intentionally can burn us deeply. Words can leave us so deeply wounded that nothing grows there. No confidence, no self-respect, no self-love, no value, no worth, no purpose, no hope, no dreams, no passion. Words can create such damage that the runoff of our heart becomes toxic, polluting the lives of those around us. Words can leave such scars that years later, after the event has long since passed and it seems as if we are over it, its effects are still evident. Without realizing it, words are still at work in our lives.

I (Kim) am a words person. Words are my number-one love language. When words are the primary way you give and receive love, they have a profound impact on you, for both good and bad. I remember many instances in elementary school when friends said critical, demeaning things that crushed my soul and wounded me deeply. Their repeated words to me were indeed like a spark that set my soul on fire and burned deeply for a long time. I was left feeling inferior and inadequate with no sense of confidence or self-worth.

As a little girl, I had no idea how to process those hurtful words, so I stuffed them down deep inside and pretended they never happened, ignoring the negative feelings. As is always the case with repression, this hurt and anger showed up in other areas of my life, and I, regretfully, used those same types of words on other people. The run-off of my heart was toxic, and it spilled over to others for many years in many ways. And even though Holy Spirit taught me to change the words I gave to others, it was years before I changed the words I gave to myself. For years I struggled with feelings of inferiority, inadequacy, and lack of confidence. Over time, as Holy Spirit healed my heart and repaired the internal damage, I realized the words those friends gave to me were not really about me. Their words to me were the toxic run-off from their own charred souls. With hindsight, this experience gave me perfect insight to the truth and wisdom of James 3:5–6.

There's no doubt; there are tremendous consequences to our words.

THE FRUIT OF THE TONGUE

> ⑥
>
> *When we indulge in our tongue, then we are going to eat the fruit of our lips.*

Let's look at Proverbs 18:21 (AMP) again: "Death and life are in the power of the tongue, And those who love it and indulge it will eat its fruit and bear the consequences of their words." As we've already mentioned, our tongue has the power to impact our lives with either death or life. But here's something else to consider: when we speak, we're producing something, and whatever we produce, we will eat. When we indulge in our tongue, then we are going to eat the fruit of our lips. The word "fruit" in this passage is the Hebrew word *peri*, and it can be translated as "earnings, products, produce, results, or rewards." We will eat what our words have produced. We will consume the earnings of our words. Our words produce consequences. Whether good or bad, we will experience the effects of our words.

Now here's where it gets good. If you go back to verse 20, it says, "A man's stomach will be satisfied with the fruit of his mouth; He will be satisfied with the consequence of his words." There are two words we want to investigate here. First, look at the word "stomach." This is the Hebrew word *beten* and it means "womb." It can also be translated as "being, inward parts, or mind."

Next, notice the word *satisfied*. In our culture, we tend to think that if we are satisfied, then we are pleased, content, or gratified. We often use it in a very positive and happy context. We like to be satisfied. It seems as if being satisfied is the ideal feeling. But the Hebrew word here is *saba* and it means "to be satisfied, filled, to be full, to have in excess, and to be sated."

To understand this Hebrew idea, picture Thanksgiving dinner. Think about eating a plate full of all your favorites, and then going back for seconds. You're indulging because it's a special occasion, and you don't have these foods every day. Think about that moment when you feel like you can't take one more bite, but you go in for the dessert sampler. You are now *excessively* full up to your chin, and you can feel your waist expanding. You waddle to the couch, get horizontal, and undo your belt. That's the meaning of the word *satisfied* in this verse.

Proverbs 18:20–21 is telling us that our words are producing something. Whatever they produce, we will have it in excess. Our beings will be overly full of the products of our words. Our minds will be stuffed with the consequences. Our inward parts engorged with the results. Our lives will burst with the earnings of our words. Those results will either produce and support life or they will produce and support death.

Since our words have such creative force, impacting our lives and the lives of others like puffs of dynamite with long-term consequence or results, Jesus told us we would have to account for every word we speak. In Matthew 12:36–37, He says, "And I tell you this, you must give an account on judgment day for every idle word you speak. The words you say will either acquit you or condemn you." We cannot wield such power without accountability.

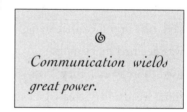

Communication wields great power.

The Greek word for "idle" is *argos*, and it means "lazy, thoughtless, unprofitable, injurious." We will give an explanation to God for every word that we were too lazy to restrain and bring under the submission of Christ. For every word that was thoughtless, insensitive, or careless. For every word that crushed, produced drama, was injurious, or brought ruin. We will be accountable for every word that supported and brought death.

THE RESPONSIBILITY OF THE TONGUE

Spiderman's Uncle Ben once said, "With great power comes great responsibility." No truer words have ever been spoken. Communication wields great power. Not only does it carry the power of life and death, it carries the weight of influence. Our idle words have the ability to sway others. Our words have the ability to pull others into truth or push them into bondage. We have the power to taint others' perspective and contaminate their opinions. Our words can turn their hearts against other people, making it difficult for them to love as Jesus loves. Our idle words can make it hard for people to see the good in situations. Our words can cause others to gravitate toward complaining. Yes, our words carry great power; therefore, we must take responsibility for them and eliminate idle words.

I (Bill) find the definition of *argos* intriguing, because the word "unprofitable" implies that words can cost you something. It also interestingly connects with the Hebrew word *peri* that is translated as "fruit" in Proverbs 18:20–21. If you'll remember, *peri* can also be translated "earnings." When I saw this, a couple of things immediately came to mind.

First, I thought of the "cuss jar." Maybe you've heard of it or participated in something like this. Or, maybe you had a teacher that made you put a quarter in a jar every time you said *ain't* or some other slang word. The idea is when you say a cuss word or a word that was deemed inappropriate, you put a designated amount of money into the jar. If you used those words, they "cost you;" therefore, it is not profitable for you to continue using those words; they created a negative experience for you.

Then, I thought of the game Scrabble. You've probably played this game. The value of the words you create is determined by adding the value of each individual letter for a total word point value. In this game, some words are more profitable than others, earning you more points. The goal is to create words that bring a high point value.

Both the cuss jar and Scrabble represent something in our lives.

Words that are idle, lazy, thoughtless, injurious, and unprofitable always create loss. Unfortunately, the loss is much more significant than losing money or a board game. Injurious words bring loss of relationships, confidence, reputations, peace, mental and emotional stability, and so much more. Thoughtless words leave a wake of destruction, with deep wounds and damage that echo throughout the course of our lives.

I wonder how many of us indulge in unprofitable words regarding ourselves, others, or our circumstances. How many of us would go broke if we had to put a dollar in the jar for every idle, lazy, thoughtless, injurious, or unprofitable word we spoke. I think we'd be shocked if an alarm alerted us every time these words rolled off our tongues.

Like Scrabble, some words have greater value than others and produce greater earnings. Words that heal, encourage, support, and bring life have great dividends. They build lives that are full and rich with peace, joy, and love. They produce relationships that are harmonious and pleasant. They create healthy self-talk that always points us back to truth.

What's interesting is that in Scrabble the word *hate* is worth seven points, and the word *love* is also worth seven points. These two words have equal value in this game, but in life if you choose to speak words of hate it will cost you and everyone involved. They fill your life with an abundance of anger, resentment, and bitterness. Hateful words are very unprofitable in life.

On the other hand, words of love are very profitable! They fill our lives with an excess of peace, joy, and happiness. Words of love produce lives filled with forgiveness, reconciliation, and restoration.

I know from experience that I would rather have a life that has an excess of love-filled words. I want my life to be bulging with the consequences of words that bring life. A life that is bursting at the seams with profitable words.

As we wrap up this chapter, take some time to inventory your words. Ask Holy Spirit to show you the produce of your words. Inspect your life to see what it's overflowing with and trace it back to the origins. You have to start some time, why not now?[2]

2

THE SCIENCE OF WORDS

Not only do words have an impact that reverberates within the soul, but they also leave a deep imprint on us physically. Let's talk about the effect words have on our body. Because this book is about complaining, we'll talk specifically about complaining and critical words. But first, we need a quick science lesson in anatomy and physiology.

Let's talk about the brain. Our brains are beautiful and complex things. Weighing approximately 2 percent of our overall body weight, this jellylike mass of fat and protein is boss, controlling everything we do. It houses our memories and gives us the capacity for rational thought and complex problem solving. It regulates breathing, temperature, blood pressure, and hormone secretions. It signals us when we are tired, hungry, or hurt. It manages movement, balance, and muscle coordination. It processes speech, hearing, vision, and information. The brain orchestrates our thoughts and physical actions, as well as regulates our unconscious processes (like breathing and heart rate), and controls the function and operation of every other organ and system in the body.

The brain does all this and so much more through billions of densely packed nerve cells called *neurons*. Through the electrical system God hardwired into our brains, neurons gather electrochemical signals and transmit them through a network consisting of millions of nerve fibers. Our brain is so highly well-organized and systematic that much of what it does goes unnoticed by you. It runs seamlessly; better than any computer ever could.

Another wonder of the brain is that God designed it for efficiency. He gave us the ability to streamline thoughts and actions for maximum productivity with minimum wasted effort. We call this gift "muscle memory," and it's like going on autopilot. We have the capacity to learn any action, and then develop the ability to repeat that action without consciously thinking about every single step required to complete the action through practice.

You currently do many things in your life through muscle memory. For example, you eat without thinking through every step of the process. You pick up a utensil, gather food with it, lift it to your mouth, place the food within your mouth, close your mouth, chew the food, and swallow. This is such an autopilot process, we had to actually think carefully about how to even write those steps.

You don't think about how to eat, you simply eat. You never think about which utensil to choose (unless you are in an up-scale restaurant with twenty-seven different utensils surrounding your plate), how to pick up the selected utensil, how to use the utensil, or how to move it into your mouth. You don't think about how to chew your food or how to swallow. You are able to do all this with no thought because you've repeated the action of eating countless times and have become extremely proficient in it. You're on autopilot when eating. It's the same idea with brushing your teeth, washing your hair, or making your bed.

In actuality, muscle memory is more about brain efficiency than it is about your muscles. Muscle memory is really an imprint on your mind, making your response time lightning fast, causing you to act before you realize.

Here's a simplified explanation of how muscle memory works (because neither one of us are scientists and we had to dumb it down for ourselves). As we noted above, your brain is full of neurons. The first time you think about something or do something, your neurons are sorting, processing, and organizing the information and experience. As you repeat the thought or behavior, the neurons in your brain notice a pattern and branch out to each other to ease the flow of information. Each time you repeat the thought or action, those neurons get closer and closer, connecting to build a permanent bridge, linking each thought and action together for fluidity and simplicity. With every repetition, that bridge is strengthened, and the connection is secured. In other words, a repeated thought or action rewires your brain so you can more efficiently accomplish that action in the future. It becomes so easy that you are able to step into that thinking pattern or perform the action with very little thought.

> ⑥
>
> *A repeated thought or action rewires your brain so you can more efficiently accomplish that action in the future.*

The scientific term for this is *neuroplasticity*. This is your brain's ability to reshape and reorganize itself. This means the brain is malleable and changes. Through the scientific technology of magnetic resonance imaging (MRI), we have the capability to clearly see the brain's ability to alter itself.

In an article, Ainslie Johnstone, DPhil student in the Wellcome Centre for Integrative Neuroimaging at Oxford University, says:

Using magnetic resonance imaging (MRI), researchers can study the many different types of changes that allow us to learn and remember a motor skill. One of these changes involves increasing the connections between the different areas of the brain that are required for a particular skill. In one study, performed in Oxford, healthy adults had MRI scans before and after six weeks of juggling training. These scans could detect white matter, the long fibres that connect different parts of the brain together. The researchers found that after the juggling training there was an increase in the white matter connections between regions of the brain responsible for vision and regions responsible for making movements.[3]

In this study, the MRI showed new neural pathways, or bridges, were created through repetition. These bridges connected different parts of the brain together, enabling the person to juggle.

So what does this scientific stuff mean to us and the subject at hand? The continual thoughts you have and the words you use are imprinting neural pathways in your brain, or creating bridges, making it much easier for you to repeat those same thoughts and step into the actions associated with those thoughts.

When you complain, the neurons in your brain notice a pattern and branch out to each other to ease the flow of information. Each time you complain, those neurons get closer and closer, connecting to build a permanent bridge, linking each complaining thought together for fluidity and simplicity. These bridges connect certain areas of the brain together, associating negativity with specific parts of our lives. With every complaint, that bridge is strengthened, and the connection is secured.

Complaining rewires your brain so that you can more easily and efficiently complain. Repeated complaining reorganizes your brain to make future complaining more likely. When you complain, your brain is restructured to find the negative first, to find fault, see the glass half empty, to look at the difficulties and impossibilities, particularly in the areas where you've established complaining.

> ⑥
> *Complaining rewires your brain so that you can more easily and efficiently complain.*

For example, if you frequently complain about your spouse, you'll find your spouse can do very little right and it's hard to see their amazing qualities. If you often grumble about your job, you find you hate it more with every passing day and it's hard to be thankful for perks and benefits of the job. In fact, you'll declare there are no perks or benefits of the job.

You see, the more we complain, the easier it becomes to see the negative, and the harder it becomes to see the positive. The result is that complaining becomes our default behavior, and we develop a pessimistic worldview. We automatically view our self, our life, our circumstances and people negatively. We then reinforce it by complaining about all the negative we see. And the vicious cycle is perpetuated.

It sounds to us like science supports the truth of Proverbs 18:20 (AMP): "A man's stomach will be satisfied with the fruit of his mouth; He will be satisfied with the consequence of his words." When you complain, your being, your mind will be stuffed and have in excess the fruit of complaining: negativity. And negativity does not support life; it contributes to death.

STRONGHOLDS

As we thought about neuroplasticity, imprinting neural pathways, and a malleable brain, it seemed to us that science has also given us proof of strongholds. What's a stronghold? It's a military term that refers to a fortress that is dominated by a group or organization and is well fortified. Strongholds are centers that control an area or region, determining what takes place in that area or region. Think of it as a command center.

Holy Spirit refers to strongholds in 2 Corinthians 10:3–4: "We are human, but we don't wage war as humans do. We use God's mighty weapons, not worldly weapons, to knock down the strongholds of human reasoning and to destroy false arguments." The spiritual strongholds mentioned here are well-fortified fortresses or command centers in our minds that are dominated by the enemy. Through the strongholds, the enemy is controlling those areas of thinking and has tremendous influence in those areas of our lives.

Strongholds are established in our minds in various ways, often through wounds we experience and lies we believe. Through these avenues, the enemy is able to secure that area in our thinking and build the fortress. It's important to note that the enemy can't build a stronghold in our minds without our permission; he is not able to build strongholds unless we allow him to; unless we help him. One of the main ways we partner with him is through our words.

Consider this: the enemy suggests that we complain about an issue or person in our lives. We know this is a suggestion of the enemy because, as children of God, complaining is not a part of our new Christlike natures. Galatians 2:20 (TPT) says:

My old identity has been co-crucified with Messiah and no longer lives; for the nails of his cross crucified me with him. And now the essence of this new life is no longer mine, for the Anointed One lives his life through me—we live in union as one! My new life is empowered by the faith of the Son of God who loves me so much that he gave himself for me, and dispenses his life into mine!

And Romans 6:11 tells us that we are dead to sin and alive in Christ. So since we are dead, it can't be us suggesting that we complain, because dead things don't make suggestions (or anything else for that matter). Jesus, the One living in us, certainly isn't giving us complaining thoughts. Therefore, it must be the enemy who shoots the fiery darts of complaining into our minds.

The enemy's motive in suggesting the complaint is not to help us resolve an issue, work through a problem, improve a situation, or help a relationship, but to gain access to our lives through a door he entices us to open. The enemy wants us to see things from his perspective and grumble so that we'll come into agreement with him. While the enemy wants to build strongholds in our minds, he is unable to do so without our cooperation. In this suggestion to complain, he's pointing to a building material for the stronghold and hoping we'll pick it up. When we fall for his scheme and start to gripe, we've entered into a partnership with him.

In essence, we are picking up the building material and handing it to the enemy so that he can continue with construction. Every time we complain, we hand the enemy another brick to reinforce his stronghold. Every time we criticize, we pass him a bucket of mortar. Through our words, we are giving him supplies to secure his position in our thinking.

> Every time we complain, we hand the enemy another brick to reinforce his stronghold.

As we grumble, the neurons get closer and closer, building a permanent bridge, linking each complaining thought together, solidifying the connection. We are building a stronghold. The neural pathways we are creating are being built in partnership with the enemy through our words. The enemy is using the neuroplasticity of our minds against us.

That's shocking, isn't it? But this is exactly why Holy Spirit warns us in Philippians 2:14 to "do everything without complaining and arguing." We often read this verse and others like it and think that God is being nitpicky. We think He's controlling, trying to micromanage every aspect of our lives. However, nothing could be farther from the truth. These are gems of wisdom given to us by a loving Father whose heart's desire is to care for us. He gives us these instructions to protect us from the strategy of the enemy, to keep us from bondage, to help us discover the depths of freedom, and enable us to experience the abundant life He died to give us. In His love for us, He says, "Do everything without complaining and arguing."

And yes, He meant everything. We know that was His intent because we looked up the word *everything* in the original text. The Greek word is *pas* and it means both "individually and collectively: each, every, any, all, the whole, everyone, all things, everything." In other words, it means all the individual pieces that make a whole *and* the whole itself. No exceptions. No limitations. No restrictions. No exclusions. No omissions. No loopholes.

That means when we make statements like these in a sarcastic, frustrated, annoyed, disgusted, whiney, or angry tone, we are handing the enemy supplies, helping him build a stronghold in our mind:

- I don't like . . .

- I wish they would/wouldn't . . .

- It makes me mad when . . .

- I hate it when . . .

- I can't stand . . .

- I'm sick of . . .

- Why do they have to . . .

- They get on my nerves . . .

- That is so annoying . . .

- That's so stupid . . .

- Why in the world would anyone . . .

- It's terrible/awful/ridiculous/absurd that . . .

When we make statements like those about any of the following, we are building a permanent bridge, linking each complaining thought together, solidifying the connection, and ensuring the longevity of the stronghold the enemy is building:

- Our self

- Our spouse

- Our kids

- Our family

- Friends

- Co-workers

- Strangers

- Work

- Salary

- Responsibilities

- Church

- Leadership

- Decisions

- Government, politicians, officials

- Changes that are implemented anywhere

- Food

- How they organize the grocery store

- How the traffic light works

- The weather

When we complain about people, and situations, whether we had any involvement in the situation or not, whether we know the person or not, we've just helped the enemy expand, and solidify, the stronghold.

Ok. It's about to get real in here.

CRITICISM

Did you know that an aspect of complaining is criticism? To criticize someone is to find fault with them. To criticize is to complain about a particular aspect of their person, efforts, decisions, or work.

This is an epidemic. It might even be our national pastime. As a society, we seem to enjoy—thrive even—on the sport of criticism. From politics to fashion, we have created a culture that loves to find fault, and ridicule everyone and everything publicly. No one is off limits. Nothing is out of bounds. We'll criticize anyone about anything. We see it on TV, in magazines, and on social media. It's found in our humor, comedy, and entertainment. It's so common, we don't recognize it anymore. In fact, it seems perfectly normal.

Criticism is so normal in our society that we've created an industry around criticizing—an official, acceptable platform for criticism. We've invented a profession whose main (though not only) job is to find fault in another's talent, skill, or abilities and publish their critique in order to notify the public of their opinion. Food critics, theater critics, movie critics, fashion critics, art critics, music critics, and sports commentators all live to share their criticisms with the world.

We are not only spectators in this sport as it plays out in the world around us; we are full-on players of the game. From family and friends, to strangers, political figures, and entertainment personalities, we'll criticize anyone and anything. And we are vicious. No matter where we are, who we're with, or what we hear or see, we have the habit of disapproving of the people and things around us. It doesn't matter if we know them or not. It doesn't matter if we have the ability to do what we are criticizing them for or not. It doesn't matter if we have any details or knowledge of the situation. Whether we think it or say it, we are ripping people to pieces as we evaluate their lives, their persons, their skills, and talents.

Social media has given us the perfect playing field for this sport. We can easily pass along harsh criticisms under the cover of a profile to people we will never see. We never see the pain in their eyes or the hurt that crosses their faces as our harsh, critical, complaints wash over them. We have dehumanized the sport with anonymity.

This is such a dangerous activity that Holy Spirit warns us against participating in it in Galatians 5:15 (MSG): "If you bite and ravage each other, watch out—in no time at all you will be annihilating each other, and where will your precious freedom be then?" The reality is, criticizing puts limits and restraints on us. It shackles us. Puts us in bondage. It just doesn't make sense to return to bondage over opinions.

> ✆
>
> *Criticizing is nothing more than having an opinion that is different from the one expressed, and then passing judgment on that different opinion in a disapproving way.*

Criticizing is nothing more than having an opinion that is different from the one expressed, and then passing judgment on that different opinion in a disapproving way. Jesus warned us of the dangers of being opinionated. In Luke 11:35 (TPT) He said, "Watch out that you do not mistake your opinions for revelation-light." There's nothing wrong with having the opinion that chocolate is better than vanilla (because it is). However, in the words of effervescent Joy from *Inside Out*, for most of us it's difficult to tell the difference between facts and opinions because they all look alike. Jesus issued this warning to us because too often we believe that what we think is the only way to see it. We believe that the way we see it is the way it is. Obviously, we are not talking about matters of Scripture. Those are superior to human reasoning and transcend opinion, though too often we pull God and the Bible into our human box and ascribe opinions to them. What we're talking about is living from the perspective that what we think about anything is the divine, supernatural disclosure to humanity, and anyone who disagrees with us doesn't have any sense.

Like Galatians 5 says, criticism leads to biting and devouring—arguing. We argue about as much as we criticize and complain. We argue *because* we criticize and complain. We debate, protest, and have heated discussions about anything and everything, all based upon our opinions. We'll fight about trivial, insignificant topics like how to put toilet paper on the toilet paper holder. We'll have heated discussions on standing or kneeling at sporting events

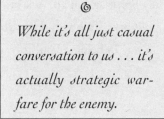

While it's all just casual conversation to us . . . it's actually strategic warfare for the enemy.

or whether elephants or donkeys should run the country. We'll even have intense conversations over the meaning of Scripture and what worship should look like. Pick any topic and it can get heated in just a matter of minutes.

The fruit of complaining, criticizing, and arguing is frustration, discouragement, unhappiness, and a host of other things. Our minds are stuffed with and have an excess of negative emotions that just keep us bogged down and feeling overwhelmed, annoyed, and frustrated, producing despair and hopelessness. We live in a perpetual state of discontent and dissatisfaction.

On top of that, all the complaining and criticizing, is ultimately helping the enemy build his fortress so he can control that area in our minds. When he controls an area, he keeps us in a pessimistic state of mind, preventing us from seeing what God is doing and hearing what God is saying. The monstrosity he's constructing keeps us from connecting to the promises of God and recognizing His blessings; it obstructs our vision so that we can't lock our sights on God's goodness or His faithfulness.

While it's all just casual conversation to us as we complain about the weather, gripe about our kids, criticize our coworkers, and argue our points, it's actually strategic warfare for the enemy. Our intent may be only to vent, but his intention is bondage by taking advantage of our lack of knowledge and exploiting our ignorance.

We hope it has been somewhat of a shocker for you to realize that complaining is actually partnering with the enemy. We've got more to say on this, but for now we encourage you to stop and think through what you've just read. We've dumped a lot of information on you in these first two chapters, and we'd like you to absorb this before you tackle the next chapter.

We encourage you not to rush through this book. Take your time and dialogue with Holy Spirit as you go. Ask Him what you need to be aware of in this chapter, and then highlight it. Talk with Him about it. Journal what He is showing you. All this will go a long way in helping you stop criticizing, quit complaining, and find abundant joy![4]

3

SILENCE THE CRITIC

While it's easy to identify the sin of criticizing others, we often miss the sin of criticizing ourselves.

I (Kim) have been known to be my own worst critic. In the past I would have worn that as a badge of honor, because in my opinion (there's that word again!), this indicated that I was good at introspection and reflection. I would diligently scrutinize my words, thoughts, attitudes, and actions, searching for anything that was less than what I deemed acceptable. I told myself this was the behavior of a responsible person. I told myself that the goal was improvement. Personal excellence. To be a better person. I was striving to be the best I could be, and my standard was set pretty high. My standard was perfection.

However, the truth is I was only trying to beat someone else to the punch. I had such a fear of rejection and critical words from others that I tried to discover all my faults first and correct them immediately. This often meant berating myself in front of others to show them I was aware of my flaws and had a handle on my issues, so there was no need for them to say anything. I said it for them. Quite firmly.

The verbal beatings didn't stop once I had addressed the issues publicly. They continued and intensified in the solitude of my mind. I was indeed my own worst critic. And the results were self-abuse.

As I harshly combed through areas of my life, I would often ridicule myself for not being enough. Of not being better or smarter at everything. I would belittle myself for not knowing better, not knowing more, not being more. I blasted myself for not accomplishing more or being further along. I rebuked myself for all the should haves, would haves, and could haves that I discovered. Regret gripped me. Condemnation crushed me. Shame smothered me. And I tried harder. The emotional baggage was substantial.

The damage was significant. Remember neuroplasticity and rewiring the malleable brain? This is exactly what I did to myself. I trained myself to perpetually see the negative in myself. Repeated criticism reorganized my brain, making future criticism more likely. By criticizing myself, I restructured my brain to find the negative about me first. I'm here to testify, it works. The cycle was vicious.

The name-calling was out of control. Stupid, ridiculous, foolish, ugly, idiot, poser, fake, failure. The list of names goes on and on. I am hard-pressed to find any name that didn't have a negative or sarcastic connotation on it.

Anytime anyone offered me a compliment, I outwardly thanked them for the kind words, but internally I immediately dismissed them. I've also been known to verbally dismiss the compliment as well. I told myself I should not hold on to those words because I didn't want pride to creep in, so I either ignored it, giving their words no consideration or appreciation, or I excused their words. I would excuse them by saying things like: they don't know me very well, they are just being nice, they have to say those things, they should have seen how awful it was last time. Those and a list of other excuses I had concocted stood ready at the helm to wipe away any words of affirmation and praise. In all honesty, no one has ever treated me as poorly as I have treated myself.

CHANGE

The tide began to turn when Holy Spirit illuminated a few key verses to me. First, I noticed Ephesians 4:29: "Don't use foul or abusive language. Let everything you say be good and helpful, so that your words will be an encouragement to those who hear them." I memorized this verse long ago as I was learning to control my tongue. I always applied it to the words I spoke to others because I wanted my words to bless others and encourage them. I never once thought to apply this truth to the words I used on myself. As a follower of Jesus, I would never say to others the things I say to myself. Never. I would never allow myself to devalue another person in the way I devalued myself.

Why did I view myself as less than others? Why did I assume those words should never be used on another but were acceptable to be used on me? The more I meditated on this, the more I began to realize God instructs me to never use foul and abusive language when I am talking to or about anyone—including me. His expectations are for every word to be good and helpful, so that my words are an encouragement to myself.

Next, I noticed Psalm 139:14: "Thank you for making me so wonderfully complex! Your workmanship is marvelous—how well I know it." This verse is very familiar to me. In fact, I love this whole psalm and soak in the verses that declare God sees me, knows me, goes before me, and follows me as He places His hand of blessing on my head. It's like a spa that renews my soul.

But I had never really let the reality of verse 14 soak into my heart. He made me. God Himself hand-crafted me. And His workmanship—His artistry—is marvelous. The word *marvelous* is the Hebrew word *pala*, and it means "to be surpassing or extraordinary." It can also be translated as "special, wonderful, and wondrously marvelous." Anything God makes is sur-

> ⑥
>
> *Should anyone ever criticize anything handcrafted by the perfect, flawless God?*

passing, extraordinary, special, and wondrously marvelous because He is perfect and never makes a mistake. Should anyone ever criticize anything handcrafted by the perfect, flawless God? Is there ever room for criticism for something that is wondrously marvelous? Even if the critic has insider information and knows about hidden issues? Probably not, because the Artist has all the same insider information and has declared it is good.

Then I saw Romans 8:1 (TPT): "So now the case is closed. There remains no accusing voice of condemnation against those who are joined in life-union with Jesus, the Anointed One." When I stepped into relationship with Jesus, the voice of my ultimate critic was silenced. Jesus stripped away every weapon and all spiritual authority from the enemy and removed his power to accuse us (Colossians 2:15 TPT). Or, we could say, his power to criticize us. So why did I insist on chiming in where the enemy had been silenced? The reality is, the enemy can no longer accuse me because I am hidden in Jesus. However, he can feed me his critical accusations, and I can repeat them. So instead of aligning myself with the enemy's perspective and speaking his language, I should be listening to the words of my loving Abba as He sings and rejoices over me (Zephaniah 3:17). Looking at things in this light certainly shifted my outlook on myself.

> ☙
>
> *The enemy can no longer accuse me because I am hidden in Jesus.*

Finally, Philippians 4:8 (MSG) caught my attention: "Summing it all up, friends, I'd say you'll do best by filling your minds and meditating on things true, noble, reputable, authentic, compelling, gracious—the best, not the worst; the beautiful, not the ugly; things to praise, not things to curse." I think this one really seals the deal for me. While I once thought this verse applied to everything *outside* of me, I began to realize His intentions were also meant for everything *inside* of me. Looking at this verse, I can honestly say that any criticism cannot be a part of a follower's vocabulary. I can clearly see that Holy Spirit is instructing me to fill my mind with things that are the best, things that are beautiful, and things to praise. And if my mind is full of those things, then there is no room for critical words, for myself or anyone or anything else.

This verse helped me to see that I needed a complete overhaul on the way I looked at myself and how I spoke to myself. In order to be spiritually, mentally, and emotionally healthy, I had to reject self-criticism. I needed to focus on the best—what I did right. I needed to concentrate on the beautiful, but not beauty according to society's standard and not just about my physical appearance. Beauty according to His standard regarding every aspect of my life. I needed to inspect for things to praise, looking for where I hit the mark, did it right, was successful.

I'm not talking about cultivating arrogance and pride or becoming vain. And, I'm certainly not talking about inflating oneself to appear better than another or valuing myself more than another. I'm also not suggesting that we ignore sin issues or let ourselves remain in dysfunctional behavior. We can't pretend we don't have issues that need addressing. What I'm saying is, we should think about ourselves the same way God thinks about us. We should see ourselves through His eyes. If we are supposed to love others like we love ourselves (Matthew 22:39), then we really need to figure this out.

INTROSPECTION

Introspection is a very important part of soul care. It's vital for spiritual growth and development. However, self-criticism is a tool the enemy uses to steal from us, kill things in our lives, and destroy us. We should never criticize ourselves. Jesus does not, so why should we?

The key is to do introspection *with* God. When we partner with Abba Father, His tender love for us affirms us and lets us know that He is pleased with us. He reminds us that He is for us and not against us (Romans 8:31). He assures us that He is on our side, working with us for our good (Psalm 118:6 and Romans 8:28).

As He affirms us, we allow Holy Spirit to search our hearts. Through His insight we can, in hope, recognize specific issues that need attention. Partnering with Him prevents us from having the hopeless sense that the whole of us is an unsalvageable mess.

In the process, we lean into Jesus and He gives us the strength to journey through correction, discipline, and change into freedom. When we do this with Him, we avoid self-criticism and discover wholeness and peace. The Bible outlines the perfect process for introspection.

First, we give God permission to examine and inspect us. Psalm 26:2 (TPT) says, "Lord, you can scrutinize me. Refine my heart and probe my every thought. Put me to the test and you'll find it's true." And Psalm 139: 23–24 (TPT) says:

God, I invite your searching gaze into my heart. Examine me through and through; find out everything that may be hidden within me. Put me to the test and sift through all my anxious cares. See if there is any path of pain I'm walking on, and lead me back to your glorious, everlasting ways— the path that brings me back to you.

We invite Him to inspect every part of our hearts. Give Him permission to probe. Dig deep. Go anywhere He wants to go. Inspect thoughts. Examine attitudes, perspectives, and perceptions. Shine His light on words. Expose motives. Show us things we don't see. Uncover things we've hidden. Things we don't even know are there. Sift through our conversations from the day and point out things that merit our attention.

> *If we listen carefully, we'll hear Him celebrating us.*

Then give Him the space to speak. Don't assume He's coming with a hammer to "criticize." That's not the heart of Abba Father. If we listen carefully, we'll hear Him celebrating us. He will applaud and encourage us, pointing out how closely we walked with Him that day and how intently we listened to Him. He'll tell us how proud He is of our successes, of our moments of obedience, surrender, and sacrifice. He'll gently convict us. He'll point out those times we got ahead of Him, misspoke, had an attitude, or had selfish motives. He never paints with broad strokes, but instead is specific, isolating the single event.

Second, we dialogue with Him about everything that surfaces. We don't bring up subjects He isn't discussing. We don't drag things out He's not addressing. We follow His lead and go only where He is going, taking in His heart on everything.

Third, we ask Him to teach us. Psalm 143:10 (AMP) says, "Teach me to do Your will [so that I may please You], For You are my God; Let Your good Spirit lead me on level ground." We need Him to teach us how to navigate through difficult situations, so we don't make the same missteps again. We need Him to instruct us on how to avoid the snares of the enemy, so we don't fall prey to his cunning schemes.

Last, we ask for revelation. Psalm 16:11 (TPT) says, "For you bring me a continual revelation of resurrection life, the path to the bliss that brings me face-to-face with you." We ask to see His perspective. To see ourselves from His point of view. To hear through His ears and see through His eyes. To see what He sees when He looks at us.

Introspection with God is a critical part of being transformed by the renewing of our minds—or we could also say, the rewiring of our brains. As we journey intimately with Him, it enables us to see ourselves clearly, through His eyes. And as we do, we begin to love ourselves like He loves us. We begin to say about ourselves what He is saying about us. And as we humbly say the best, beautiful, and praiseworthy things about ourselves, we rewire our brains so that we can more easily and efficiently affirm ourselves. This repeated affirmation also reorganizes our brains to make future affirmation more likely because we're restructuring our brains to find the best, beautiful, and praiseworthy things about us.

I'm here to testify it works. I am still in the process, but I have discovered this new cycle is both victorious and beautiful. And it's a much better way to live.

4

OPINIONS ARE LIKE ONIONS

In light of what we wrote in chapter 2, we can hear what many of you are thinking: *Are you saying I can't have opinions? I can never express my opinions? I can't tell anyone what I think? Ever? Am I just supposed to be an emotionless Vulcan⁵ who doesn't care about what's happening around me? To me? How do you expect me to deal with legitimate problems? Frustrating people? Painful situations? Am I supposed to be silent about the negative things around me? Injustices I see? I can't talk about the difficulties and struggles I am experiencing?*

We know you are thinking that because we've thought those same things. Struggled with those same ideas as Jesus led us along in this journey. We are not saying you should not have opinions. We are not saying you can't express your opinions or that you must be a silent victim to things going on around you or to you. We are not saying you can't point out something that isn't right. We aren't saying that you can't process through difficult situations with the help of another. And we aren't saying you need to eliminate opinions altogether.

But let's be honest about it. Often our opinions are nothing more than complaints and critiques of someone else. The only reason we have some opinions is because we don't like what we see or hear.

I (Kim) remember strolling through a quaint downtown area with Bill one day. It was one of those rare days where we could just get away and do nothing. As we meandered through the streets, we passed a certain structure, and I internally commented on the architecture of the building, thinking: *How silly. Why would they design it this way? They should have constructed it this way instead of that way.* Immediately Holy Spirit spoke to me, gently pointing out the criticalness of my internal commentary. He asked me if I would volunteer this information to those responsible for the design, at the risk of hurting their feelings. I immediately responded no, because at once I saw they would have been pleased with their work and efforts, honored to have made a long-standing contribution to the community. My critical comments, even off-handed, would have been hurtful.

He then asked if the building or its design had eternal significance. Again, I responded no, because in the grand scheme of things, Jesus will not ask me about that building when I see Him in Heaven (though He will ask me about a critical heart). He then asked me why I needed an opinion on this subject. I responded, I don't. And with that, off came another layer of Kim and I gained more understanding of the Father's heart.

You see, most of our complaints and criticisms are just the expression of our opinions that are not necessarily based upon fact but are shaped by preferences. We complain about the weather because we prefer something different. We criticize strangers because we don't like what we see. We critique another's choices because we would choose something different. We grumble about the government because we think things should be done according to our philosophies. We express displeasure about things over which we have no control or involvement. We formed an opinion only because we didn't like what we felt, saw, or heard. Even if it seems harmless (like complaints about the weather or building designs), it's not.

A common misconception is that we must have an opinion about everything, we must tell everyone that opinion, and everyone should agree with our opinion. There's nothing wrong with having opinions on some things. But honestly, we don't need to form opinions about everything, especially if we are not involved or affected by it in any way. And we certainly don't need to develop opinions that would be hurtful to another.

The need to constantly develop opinions about anything and everything places us in the perfect position to complain and criticize because few things align with our personal preferences. We don't need opinions on the whiteness of someone's teeth, their hair color, how often they should mow their lawn, how they should spend their money, or the strategy they should have used in the game. Just because we live in the land of free speech doesn't mean we have to freely give a speech on every subject at every opportunity.

Think of all the time and energy we invest into forming these opinions. Think of all the mental real estate these opinions take up. Think of the wasted passion we expend on defending opinions that have no eternal significance. Think of all the arguments that stem from differences of opinion. Think of all the relationships broken by an unwavering opinion. And think of how you would feel if someone was forming those same opinions about you, sharing them with others, posting them on social media, or sharing them with strangers at the water cooler. Imagine yourself being the negative subject of another's thoughts and conversations.

> ⑥
>
> *Just because we live in the land of free speech doesn't mean we have to freely give a speech on every subject at every opportunity.*

Proverbs 18:2 reminds us, "Fools have no interest in understanding; they only want to air their own opinions." The fewer opinions we have regarding things that really don't matter, the less critical we will be. Let's save our mental real estate for thoughts that support life.

Before you form an opinion (or even as you're forming an opinion), ask Holy Spirit if you really need an opinion for that situation. Yes, really. It's part of living a Spirit-led life. Galatians 5:25 tells us, "Since we are living by the Spirit, let us follow the Spirit's leading in every part of our lives." Opinions are a part of our lives, so ask Him if you need one. If one is not needed, let it go and move on. But, if one is needed, ask Him to help you form it through His perspective so that you see the situation clearly. If it needs to be expressed, ask Him to help you wrap those words in love so that you speak it from the position of His heart. This goes a long way in helping us defeat a critical spirit.

VENTING VS PROCESSING

Now, what do we do with difficult, painful, complicated, or frustrating situations? How do we deal with the disappointed, resentful, irritated, impatient, and angry thoughts? If we aren't supposed to complain, how do we handle the emotions and thoughts swirling in our minds? Is the answer to just keep our mouths shut?

No: you must process them. Unfortunately, we are generally not very good at processing. We usually fall into one of two camps: The first is Camp Broadcast, where venting is the primary form of communication. The second is Camp Denial, where repression is preferred over communication.

At Camp Broadcast, we aren't really processing. We're just venting. We tell everybody everything we think about everything and everyone. How we feel is no secret. No one ever has to wonder what's on our mind, because we'll complain to anyone who will listen, whether we know them or not. Friends, family, co-workers, neighbors, our hair stylists, and the lady at Walmart all know how difficult our lives are, how terrible our kids are, how rotten our ex is, and how much we despise the government. We just have to get it off our chests and we don't care who knows. We live on repeat, telling the same saga with new episodes everyday to everybody.

Over in Camp Denial, difficult people and complicated situations are too stressful to deal with. So, it's easier to ignore them altogether. Some think that following Jesus means we aren't supposed to have difficulties and therefore we can't talk about frustrations or struggles. And there are those who have misunderstood the instructions of Holy Spirit and think that doing everything without complaining and arguing means we can't express the myriad of emotions that run rampant through our minds, and we should hide those emotions. Worse yet, some pretend we don't have them. But nothing could be further from the truth. There are few things as damaging to us spiritually, mentally, emotionally, and physically than repressed emotions.

We understand why people prefer to live in Camp Denial. Sometimes it's just easier to ignore situations and live in denial instead of dealing with them openly. It can be exhausting to work through the tidal wave of feelings that rush over us, especially when they are negative. It can also be intimidating and messy to sort through problematic situations with complicated people, especially if you tend to be non-confrontational. For those who hang out at Camp Denial, sharing with another is often terrifying because we are afraid of judgement, criticism, and gossip. It seems like a good idea to ignore, deny, repress, and compartmentalize those emotions, shutting them off in those areas of our lives. If we don't feel the stress of a problem, we won't have to deal with the problem.

What we fail to realize is we really can't compartmentalize our emotions. If we attempt to shut them off in one area, we've affected the flow in every area. Even though we've tried to hide or push down what we feel, those emotions are still there, bubbling beneath the surface, usually in the form of complaining. Instead of confronting our spouses about an issue, we gripe about them in our minds. Instead of tackling a problem with our bosses, we criticize their leadership skills, knowledge, or qualifications to our co-workers. Instead of addressing concerns we have with those involved in our situation, we nitpick and speculate motives and intentions with a third party. Instead of dealing with the repeat offenders in our lives, we make subtle digs and inject sarcasm into our conversations with them.

It's going to come out somewhere. We may repress so deeply that we begin to complain about completely unrelated things. We may have hidden our thoughts, feelings, and opinions from those involved in our situation, but they seep out (or even erupt) with others in other areas.

Repressing our emotions is very unhealthy for us mentally, physically, and spiritually. It builds walls between ourselves and others. Worse yet, it builds walls between ourselves and God. It isolates us and causes the negative chatter in our minds to increase significantly. We may prevent our thoughts and emotions from flowing out in one area, but they will explode in another, damaging us and everyone within reach.

When Holy Spirit instructed us to do everything without complaining or arguing, He did not mean for us to ignore issues. Father God did not hardwire us to live in denial. He hardwired us for communication. If we find ourselves in difficult situations, dealing with challenging people or repeat offenders, and we feel disappointed, or resentful— then we should talk about it. We need to talk about it. We need to process through the rough patch and difficult season through communication.

So, where's the balance? How do we live in between the two camps at Camp Healthy?

FIRST, PROCESS WITH JESUS

He is our first line of defense. He is our best friend, the One who sticks closer than a brother. No one understood this better than David. Living on the run from King Saul, separated from his family, living in a cave and fearing for his life, David certainly had opportunity to vent—reason to vent. However, he knew that processing troubles with God was the only way he could survive the difficulties he faced. So, in his pain and frustration, he cried out to God. Psalm 142:1–2 reveals how he responded in times of trouble: "I cry out to the LORD; I plead for the LORD's mercy. I pour out my complaints before him and tell him all my troubles."

David poured out all his complaints, frustrations, disappointments, and fears directly to God. He processed everything he felt and thought with God. He was able to do this because he knew—he was confident—God would hear his cries and respond. He testified to this in Psalm 18:6 (TPT): "I cried out to you in my distress, the delivering God, and from your temple-throne you heard my troubled cry. My sobs came right into your heart and you turned your face to rescue me."

With that kind of testimony, why wouldn't we want to process with Jesus?! No one understands us better than Him. Holy Spirit reveals how intimately He knows us in Psalm 139:1–4 (TPT):

> Lord, you know everything there is to know about me. You perceive every movement of my heart and soul, and you understand my every thought before it even enters my mind. You are so intimately aware of me, LORD. You read my heart like an open book and you know all the words I'm about to speak before I even start a sentence! You know every step I will take before my journey even begins.

Isn't that amazing? He understands us and identifies with our emotions and experiences. He even understands us when we don't understand ourselves. He knows why we think and feel the way we do even when we don't understand why.

Processing with God isn't a sign of weakness or failure. There isn't anything wrong with us because we need to process. David certainly wasn't weak, and there wasn't anything wrong with him. He was simply doing what he was created to do. This is how God designed us to handle stress, problems, and difficulties. Holy Spirit knew we would need encouragement to process things with Jesus, so in 1 Peter 5:7 (AMP), He recommends "casting all your cares [all your anxieties, all your worries, and all your concerns, once and for all] on Him, for He cares about you [with deepest affection, and watches over you very carefully]."

There is such relief and freedom in casting your cares on Jesus. I (Kim) had a lot of processing sessions during the Blight of '17. One particular moment was when the purchase of the first house we'd made an offer on fell through. It seemed to be the perfect house. We really liked this home and could easily see ourselves

> ©
>
> *There is such relief and freedom in casting your cares on Jesus.*

living there. The neighborhood was beautiful. The lawn was beautiful. The architecture of the home was beautiful. Everything was beautiful. Hope had sprung up in our hearts, and we began to anticipate the possibilities and see light at the end of the tunnel.

Imagine our deep disappointment when that house failed inspection. It was almost tangible. We were shocked. We stood in their beautiful home and looked at each other, speechless, as tears filled our eyes. We were looking at homes during the Christmas season, so the selection was very small. There wasn't anything else on the market that fit our price point and met our needs. We were crushed.

We left that house and went to our temporary dwelling, the apartment in the Brown's warehouse. This is where we realized that disappointment is the breeding ground for complaining, and criticizing. Complaining words were hanging on the tips of our tongues, anxious to leap out. We rode home in silence. It was hard, but we eventually made the conscious decision to thank Jesus for revealing those issues to us before it was too late instead of complaining.

I'll admit, I had a more difficult time than Bill did. He seemed to latch on to peace pretty quickly, but I continued to wrestle with this disappointment internally and felt as if complaining was going to erupt from my soul like a volcanic explosion. I just didn't understand. It was so unexpected. It didn't make sense.

During the night, Jesus woke me up and encouraged me to process with Him so that He could help me work through this setback. I crept into the living room under the cover of darkness, and wrapped in a blanket, I poured my heart out to Him. I told Him how much I loved that house. I wanted *that* house. I told Him how perfectly it fit our family. I told Him I was terrified that we would not find a home for months and that we would take advantage of our gracious hosts. I told Him there were no other homes to choose from. I sobbed and talked. Then talked and sobbed. And then, I listened.

In the quiet, He simply asked if I would place that house, my desires, and my disappointment in His hands. He asked me for surrender. He did not remove the desire for that house from my heart. He asked me to trust and surrender the desire to Him. It's easy to let go of something you don't really want. It's a completely different story to let go of something you want badly. This was not easy for me, but I chose to do it. And I had to do it several times as it took time for my heart to catch up with my head. But with each opportunity, I chose to process with Him using words of thanksgiving and praise. Together, He and I navigated through this setback.

So, we encourage you to lay in His lap and pour your heart out. Tell Him everything you think and feel. Be real and honest. You don't have to pretend with Him. You don't have to clean it up for Him. If you're angry, frustrated, disgusted, or fed-up, tell Him. If you don't like something or are unhappy with someone, tell Him. Spill your guts. Get it all out. Since He knows all the words you're about to speak before you even start a sentence, you won't surprise Him by your admission. He won't be shocked by your raw honesty or intense emotions. He won't shame you or tell you that you shouldn't feel that way. He already knows everything going on inside of you. You're not talking to Him for the purpose of informing Him. You're talking to Him for the purpose of freeing yourself. So, don't worry if it gets messy; He can handle it. Let Him help you sort through it all. He will meet you right where you are with love, tenderness, and comfort for your soul.

SECOND, LISTEN

Then, after you've poured it all out, listen. Too often we do the talking but forget to do the listening. But listening is at the heart of processing. It's the part where peace, strength, and hope enter the picture. If you only talk, you're still venting, just to Jesus. It becomes processing when you are willing to listen and apply His wisdom.

So, get still in His arms. As He holds you, He will whisper words of peace, wisdom, correction, and direction into your heart to help you navigate through this rough spot. He will help you see your circumstances through His eyes, hear people through His ears, and feel with His heart. Processing with Jesus produces change in me. It shifts my perspective. It gives me clarity and insight that I can't get any other way. It cultivates mercy and increases compassion because it tunes my ears into His frequency.

Depending on your situation, you may need to do this frequently (daily, even!) and that's all right. There's no one better to process with than Jesus and He never grows weary of helping us!

When we take every opinion, complaint, and criticism to Jesus, He helps us sort through what is really important and what merits our attention and emotional energy. We will naturally let some complaints and opinions go as we tell Jesus about them because we'll realize those are non-issues as we step into His presence.

In addition to processing with Jesus, there are times we may need to process with a human. It's okay to find a friend or confidant who will listen to you sort through emotions and separate lies from truth. However, we need to be wise in who we share with. Don't just choose a warm body, but selectively choose someone you can trust, who is spiritually sound and can objectively listen. Choose someone who will always remind you of truth (not their opinion) and who will pray with you. Be sure they will be straightforward and direct with you—you don't need a "yes man." You want someone who is strong in the area you are struggling with. Don't discuss marriage issues with someone who always complains about their spouse or marriage. Don't talk about the problems you have with your boss at work with someone who criticizes their boss or hates their job.

Talk with the wise friend openly and honestly, allowing them to be open and honest with you in return. Give them permission to point out what you may be missing or what you can't see. Ask them to help you see things from a different perspective, even if it's painful to hear. Proverbs 27:6 (TPT) says, "You can trust a friend who wounds you with his honesty," and Proverbs 28:23 (MSG) says, "In the end, serious reprimand is appreciated far more than bootlicking flattery." Hearing what they have to say may be difficult and could sting, but direct and honest feedback is spiritually healthy for you. Then, take all they had to say and continue processing with Jesus.

Processing is a much healthier option than venting. While the purpose of processing is to move into a better emotional state, to protect and preserve relationships, to resolve conflict, to solve problems, and to experience greater spiritual freedom, venting is all about emotionally vomiting on anyone who will listen. If your purpose is to simply vent, you'll only want people who will validate your feelings and agree with your perspective, someone who will side with you. When you vent, the only feedback wanted is an endorsement of your position. In reality, venting is just complaining for the sake of complaining.

HOW DO YOU KNOW IF YOU ARE PROCESSING OR VENTING?

First, ask yourself if this is an ongoing conversation. Do you find you're having the same conversation with different people continually? Do you hear yourself saying the same things over and over, like a broken record? Are you progressing toward resolution? Are you gaining clarity? Getting healthier? Processing has a beginning and an end. Venting is just an ongoing conversation we have on repeat.

Next, check your motives. Before you start to talk about it, ask why you are talking about it. What is your purpose for expressing your thoughts with this person? What is your objective? What is the goal of the conversation? What do you hope to gain through the encounter? Do you honestly want to see where you've gotten off track and are willing to be course corrected? Are you willing to be corrected? Are you expressing your feelings and opinions because you are part of the solution and you're working through the challenges of the problem to produce change? Are you sincerely working toward resolution? Do you have the power or authority to bring solutions or implement change in this situation you want to discuss?

Or, are you talking about it just to talk about it? Are you saying it because it feels good to voice your opinion? Do you just want someone to know what was said or done to you? Are you saying it because it makes you feel better about yourself to criticize someone else? Are you discussing it because you want them to dislike the person you're having difficulties with? Are you talking about it because you want them to defend you? Are you trying to build alliances? Is the purpose to taint the listener's perspective? A listening ear that doesn't provide biblical input is just a venting session, which is complaining in disguise. And it's sin.

While we're on the subject, let's talk about conversations with our spouses. Often, we think that anything said within the privacy of our marriage is "legal." You may feel this about a sibling or a parent as well. However, Jesus does not view it the same way. The person you're talking to is irrelevant. Venting is not healthy. Unless you are processing and

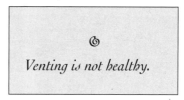

Venting is not healthy.

you follow the steps noted above, it's an inappropriate conversation. And as we stated in chapter 1, your words could negatively influence them, making it difficult for them to love others and see situations clearly.

Once your healthy processing conversation is done, check your motives again. Did you give them room to speak or did you do all the talking? Did you discount what they said because you didn't like what they said? Did you dismiss their comments because you think they don't understand? Were you offended? Offense is the number one indicator that your motives may not have been in the right place to begin with. If we honestly want to process, we will not pick up offense easily, but will be willing to hear what we've given our listener permission to say. It may sting, it might be uncomfortable, it might not be what we'd hoped to hear, but we will not be offended.

One more thing before we wrap up this chapter: there are times you will need to give feedback. There will be times you need to alert someone to a problem or point out a mistake. You may need to discuss difficulties in a relationship, address issues at work, or give comments to a service provider. Giving feedback is an opportunity to share your review and assessment of a situation. It is not an opportunity to criticize or grumble. Sharing feedback is done in the spirit of helping, encouraging, and benefiting a person or situation. As you share, don't attempt to camouflage criticism in feedback. Always be honest. But always do it in love and in a tone and spirit that you would appreciate receiving feedback in as well.

We've given you a lot to think about here. Before you move on, take some time to reflect on what you've just read. Ask Holy Spirit what camp you usually hang out in and why you are comfortable there.

5

IT'S DEMO DAY

So far, we've seen that complaining words have a creative force that not only reverberates within the soul, but also deeply impacts us physically by rewiring our brains with the construction of strongholds. Now the question is, what do we do about it? How do we stop partnering with the enemy to build strongholds? Can we tear down the strongholds that have already been established? Can we stop the cycle of complaining, criticizing, and arguing? Can we establish new bastions of truth that govern our thinking?

In the words of Jesus, "Humanly speaking, it is impossible. But with God everything is possible" (Matthew 19:26). It is impossible to demolish strongholds and push the enemy out of your life on your own. Producing life-long change apart from God is impossible. But *with* God, *everything* is possible. The word "everything" in this passage is the same Greek word we looked at in chapter 2, *pas*. In case you forgot, let us refresh your memory: it means "both individually and collectively: each, every, any, all, the whole, everyone, all things, everything." In other words, it is all the individual pieces that make a whole *and* the whole itself. No exceptions. No limitations. No restrictions. No exclusions. No omissions. No loop holes. It doesn't matter how long you've been complaining and criticizing, how often you argue, how enormous this stronghold is in your life, how steeped you are in negativity, or whether pessimism seems to be your native tongue, *with* God this thing doesn't stand a chance.

So, the obvious answer is to change partners. We've been partnering with the enemy through our words. Now, we need to use our words to partner with Jesus, our Deliverer. And when we do, those strongholds will come crumbling down, brick by brick.

HUMBLE BEFORE GOD

We start by humbling ourselves before God. Humbling means we admit that God has not been at the center of this area of our lives and we haven't allowed Him to be our source. We've been living as if we were the center, allowing things that displeased, irritated, or frustrated us to influence our attitudes, thoughts, words, and actions. We've been permitting the enemy to be the source as he fueled those dissatisfied thoughts and set our minds ablaze with complaints and criticisms (the "fiery darts" described in Ephesians 6).

When we humble ourselves, we can trust Jesus to give us the grace we need to overcome. James 4:6–7 says, "And he gives grace generously. As the Scriptures say, 'God opposes the proud but gives grace to the humble.' So humble yourselves before God. Resist the devil, and he will flee from you."

> ⑥
>
> *A function of grace in our lives is divine enablement.*

God opposes those who think they can do it by themselves, but He generously and freely pours grace into those who know they need Him and are utterly dependent on Him for everything. He lavishes grace on those who realize they can do nothing without Him. He provides an unrestricted, unlimited supply to those who draw from Him as the source of everything they are and do.

Understanding this is crucial to the destruction of strongholds in our lives. Most of us understand that grace is the unmerited favor we have with God. He extends grace to us, not only welcoming us into His Kingdom but adopting us as sons and daughters with full benefits and privileges, even though we have done nothing to earn or merit such a wonderful reception and royal treatment. But often, we think that's where grace begins and ends, and we miss the role of grace in our lives. A function of grace in our lives is divine enablement. Look at these verses that emphasize this reality:

- "So let us come boldly to the throne of our gracious God. There we will receive his mercy, and we will find grace to help us when we need it most." (Hebrews 4:16).

- "Jesus Christ is the same yesterday, today, and forever. So do not be attracted by strange, new ideas. Your strength comes from God's grace, not from rules about food, which don't help those who follow them." (Hebrews 13:8–9)

- "Timothy, my dear son, be strong through the grace that God gives you in Christ Jesus." (2 Timothy 2:1)

Did you see it? Grace to help. Strength that comes from grace. Be strong through grace. These verses reveal that the work of grace is the unmeasurable strength of God that not only pulled us out of the pit but can also keep us from returning to the pit. You see, the function of grace is to give us power. Strength for the battle. Endurance for growing seasons. The muscle to go through difficult times. Help to overcome temptation.

Grace provides you with sustainability, so you won't quit but will endure to the end. It empowers you to stay the course, giving you the ability to go against the flow of society and completely disconnect from cultural norms that are damaging to your life. Grace is the muscle of God in your life that provides you with the means, the strength, and the force to do what you could not otherwise do. It is the power to live differently every day—not just for a few moments here and there, but continuously. His grace at work in your life enables you to not just survive, but to thrive!

When you make God the center, when you confess that you are stuck in a complaining, criticizing, and argumentative rut and can't change without Him, when you acknowledge that you are dependent on Him for every aspect of change—even in the smallest detail that seems achievable in your own strength and ability—He pours out divine strength and supernatural power. And by *pour*, we mean *deluge*. Monsoon. Tsunami. He pours it out until you are drowning in it and then pours out more. And He never stops.

He is so generous and lavish with grace because He knows you need it. He knows you can't do any of this on your own. He knows you don't have the strength to produce change, free yourself, or tear down a stronghold. When you step into agreement with Him on this, He extravagantly pours strength and power into your life, enabling you to live in the victory He died to give you. Instead of relying on your own strength and resources to produce change, you can draw deeply from God's limitless grace. He becomes the power source in this area of your life, fueling thoughts of thankfulness and praise, setting your mind ablaze with gratitude and joy as you build a fortress of righteousness together. Humility taps us into the divine, unlimited grace of God, which propels us into change.

> *Humility taps us into the divine, unlimited grace of God, which propels us into change.*

The beauty of this is that when we place God at the center of an area, the enemy must evacuate that area. Resist the enemy by placing God at the center, and the enemy will flee. Our act of humility serves the enemy with an eviction notice, demanding he leave as God takes up immediate residence. Light and dark cannot co-exist, and the Light dispels the darkness every time. The enemy is now officially a trespasser and has no legal rights to operate from that stronghold in your life, so he's gotta go.

SURRENDER AND SUBMISSION

After we've humbled ourselves, we must surrender and submit. Since God now has the center position in our lives, we need to give Him permission to reign. We allow Him to be the sole influence of our attitudes, thoughts, words, and actions—to speak truth into every aspect of our lives.

However, *surrender* and *submission* are scary words. The whole concept of surrender and submission flies in the face of western civilization because freedom is everything to us. It's the drum beat of humanity, the demand of society, and the cry of the human heart. Freedom is considered the most valuable thing we possess. Wars have been fought, declarations have been written, and governments overthrown all for the sake of freedom. This deep longing for freedom compelled founding father Patrick Henry to passionately proclaim,

"Give me liberty or give me death!"[6] Humanity yearns for freedom because freedom means that we are uncontrolled, unrestrained, and unrestricted by any outward influence.

Surrender and submission terrify us because they indicate a loss: Loss of power. Loss of position. Loss of control. Loss of rights. Loss of privileges. Loss of freedom. It means we relinquish control to another and bow to their desires and direction. We refuse to be controlled or influenced by an external force. Instead, we believe that freedom comes when we throw off all restraint and live according to our own ideas, precepts, and terms. We don't want guidelines, instructions, or parameters because we view them as another's attempt to control us. We believe it will limit or restrict us, stifling us and smothering our personalities, preventing us from discovering life and expressing ourselves.

Actually, we would agree with that . . . if we are talking about a human. However, God is not human and does not think or act like humans. God is the author, giver, and source of freedom. In Galatians 5:1, Holy Spirit tells us exactly what God had in mind when He sent Jesus to rescue us: "Let me be clear, the Anointed One has set us free—not partially, but completely and wonderfully free! We must always cherish this truth and stubbornly refuse to go back into the bondage of our past" (TPT). God has always intended for us to live in freedom.

God does not want to control us. Jesus did not come to limit, restrict, or repress us. We were already limited. We were in bondage. We were slaves to sin, our flesh, and the enemy. We were bound in every possible way. Jesus didn't come to take away our freedom; we never had freedom. He came to set us free so that we could be free. He came to set us free because that was His intent all along.

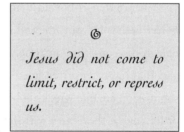

Jesus did not come to limit, restrict, or repress us.

Knowing that we don't know how to live in freedom, however, He wants to help us stay free. He gave us guidelines and principles for optimal living. He gave us parameters to live in to protect our freedom. It's not about control, it's about protection and empowerment. If God were about control, He would have never given humanity free will. He would have never given us the ability to choose anything. But He knows when we are left to our own devices, we will choose options that will enslave us again. He knows we will gravitate toward things that will imprison us, because that's all we know. That's how we've always lived, and we don't realize there's something so much better. So in His love and care for us, He tells us things like Philippians 2:14: "Do everything without complaining and arguing," to help us stay free and enjoy life.

True freedom can never be found in embracing or indulging in complaining, or criticizing. Freedom of speech does not produce freedom of the heart and mind. That only leads to bondage. Freedom is found in relinquishing our right to an opinion, letting go of our viewpoints, and trading in our thoughts, perceptions, philosophies, and worldview, in exchange for His perspective. We surrender ours and submit to His.

> ⑥
> *Freedom of speech does not produce freedom of the heart and mind.*

If you want to be free, if you want to dismantle the stronghold of the enemy, then fully surrender and completely submit. The most powerful form of warfare is surrender. The greatest weapon in your arsenal is submission. Not only is this true for complaining and criticizing, it's true for any issues you're struggling with in your life. If you need to experience victory, surrender and submit. This powerful duo does more damage to the forces of darkness than you can ever imagine.

A heart that is bowed before God in humility completely strips the enemy of any power he has in your life and it blocks his access to that area of your life. It also puts a halt in his construction zone. He loses all influence and must vacate—flee from—the area that has been surrendered and operates in submission. On top of that, surrender and submission are like wrecking balls that pummel any stronghold; regardless of size, shape, or longevity, they can't withstand the force of surrender and submission. Nothing the enemy constructed can bear the intensity of these powerful actions.

HUMBLE BEFORE OTHERS

Then, after surrender and submission to God, we must humble ourselves to each other. Philippians 2:3 (TPT) says, "Be free from pride-filled opinions, for they will only harm your cherished unity. Don't allow self-promotion to hide in your hearts, but in authentic humility put others first and view others as more important than yourselves." It's hard to complain about someone you've humbled yourself to. When you live others-focused, your thoughts are on what they think, how they feel, and what they need. By putting them first and esteeming them, you are more concerned with their spiritual, mental, and emotional well-being than you are with airing your opinions, criticizing them, or arguing your point.

We won't lie. This one is hard. Living in authentic humility toward another human just goes against the grain of the "me first" mentality of our society. Our culture encourages us to indulge ourselves and insists we can have it our way because we deserve it. Our culture makes everything all about "me." But it's completely opposite in the Kingdom of God. In the Kingdom, it's all about others. We are instructed to love others, serve others, honor others, and bless others—putting them before ourselves. If we are going to obliterate this stronghold in our thinking and live in freedom, we're going to have to walk in humility in every area of our lives, and that includes humility toward other people.

Freedom is found as we embrace the heart of God, His thoughts, His perspective, and His ways. Freedom is found in living like Jesus. It is found in loving like Him and valuing others like He does. And as we adopt this way of life, the stronghold of the enemy comes down and the bridges of negativity built in our mind are destroyed, as we simultaneously establish bridges of hope and joy and build a fortress of truth.

That's the amazing part of a malleable brain. We may have used words of complaining and criticism to partner with the enemy and build neuropathways of negativity that establish a stronghold, but we can change the words we speak and partner with God to undo all that was done and build new neuropathways of gratitude that establish a fortress of truth. Just like repeated complaining rewires your brain for negativity, repeatedly speaking truth rewires your brain for praise, thanksgiving, and gratitude.

When your brain has been rewired for praise, thanksgiving, and gratitude, you can more easily and efficiently express praise, thanksgiving, and gratitude. Repeating truth reorganizes your brain to make future thankfulness more likely. When you speak words of gratitude, your brain is restructured to find the positive first, clearly see the great qualities, see the glass half full, and look at the potential and possibilities, particularly in the areas where you've established gratitude. It becomes easy to see the positive and hard to see the negative. The result is that thankfulness becomes our default behavior and we develop an optimistic worldview. We automatically view ourselves, our lives, our circumstances, and other people from God's perspective because we surrender our perspective and submit to His. We then reinforce it by expressing thankfulness for all the positive we see. And the victorious cycle begins.

Prior to the Blight of '17, we had spent several months discussing this topic and going through two Challenges. During that time, we had many opportunities to implement what we were learning. As we mentioned, I (Bill) had months of unexplained illness that baffled doctors. There were a lot of appointments, theories, and prescriptions, none of which brought any resolution or much relief. We would Band-Aid one issue and another would crop up. With each passing month, I felt worse and worse with no end in sight. During this time, Holy Spirit began to address the issues of complaining in our lives. I became intentional in my thoughts and words, purposefully choosing words of truth and thankfulness. I didn't always succeed, but I made the continuous effort to speak life. Some days it was a tremendous battle. Some days I made myself say it out loud so I could hear those words. It was like changing the direction of a freighter, slow and steady. But by the time the mold and formaldehyde were discovered, we had made significant headway in rewiring our brains and in dismantling the stronghold of complaining. We were spiritually and mentally positioned for thankfulness and praise, and it made a huge difference in our journey as we were already beginning to be full of peace, joy, and contentment.

The same will be true for you. It will be difficult. It will be a slow process, but as you choose to think and express thankfulness, gratitude, and praise, you'll find that your life has an excess of joy, peace, contentment, and happiness. You'll see opportunities instead of obstacles. You'll see the promise and provision instead of the problem. Your circumstances may not have changed, but your hope will overflow.

To finish this chapter out, we want you to do a little ruminating. This is one of my (Kim) favorite exercises and I talk about it all the time. The perfect example of rumination is found in the cow. It's kinda gross, but it so wonderfully depicts this mental process in humans. For the cow, *rumination* is the process where previously consumed food is returned to the mouth and chewed for a second time. (I told you it was gross.) This returned, or regurgitated, food is called the cud. This breaks down the food for better digestion so that the stomach can fully absorb all the nutrients. It is said that the average cow spends eight hours a day chewing cud.

We want you to spend some time doing the same thing. You've read this chapter once. Think about it for a bit and then read it again. Investigate the word *grace*. You're going to need a lot of it as you work your way through the Challenge. *Grace* is a word we toss around in Christianity but few of us have a firm grasp on what it means. Spend some time meditating on it. Turn it over and over in your mind. Mentally chew on it so you can digest it properly.

What does grace mean in your life? How does connecting with grace change struggles for you? Go back and read the verses we shared about grace. Ask Jesus to open your mind to these Scriptures like He did for the disciples on the road to Emmaus in Luke 24. Journal what you see and pray the revelation into your heart and mind.

6

THE EXTRA MILE

I (Kim) was washing my hair one day when a revelation for the cure to chronic complaining dawned on me. For years I had been trying to rectify my complaining problem by stopping the words of complaint and criticism. When they came to mind, I would bite my tongue, determine not to say them, and keep my opinion to myself. Then, I would try to shift my attention to something else. This meant I would ignore things that irritated or annoyed me. I would close my eyes to things, situations, and people that I would like to complain about and criticize. I would put blinders on, blocking out everything because I did not want to criticize or complain. I was attempting to live by the principle of Thumper's daddy in *Bambi*: "If you can't say something nice, don't say nothing at all."[7] While it sounds good, it's only part of the equation. Yes, we shouldn't say or think complaining, critical, or negative words. But there's more to it than just zipping our lips and ignoring what's going on around us.

This *aha!* moment that unfolded as I shampooed was sponsored by a frequent teaching of Bill's. As I pondered it, a whole new perspective opened up for me and I began to see how I could break free from the sin of complaining and criticism. I'll let him explain.

My (Bill's) favorite book of the Bible is Matthew, and my favorite section in Matthew is the Sermon on the Mount, chapters 5–7. Everything you'll ever need for a rich and satisfying life is stuffed inside Jesus's most famous sermon. One of the verses I talk about frequently is Matthew 7:12: "Do to others whatever you would like them to do to you. This is the essence of all that is taught in the law and the prophets."

This verse has been labeled the Golden Rule, and most every religion has their own version of it. However, most have a slightly different twist than Jesus's teaching. For example:

- Buddhism teaches: "Treat not others in ways that you yourself would find hurtful."[8]

- Hinduism teaches: "This is the sum of duty: do not do to others what would cause pain if done to you."[9]

- Bahá'í teaches: "Lay not on any soul a load that you would not wish to be laid upon you, and desire not for anyone the things you would not desire for yourself."[10]

I could list more, but you get the point. While their philosophy sounds good, it's just as incomplete as the instructions Thumper got from his daddy. It's missing the power-packed punch—the life-changing element.

You see, what makes Jesus's teaching on this so revolutionary and powerful is that it's a call to action, not a command to refrain. While their instructions are to "don't," Jesus teaches us to "do."

It's a common thread woven all throughout this sermon. You see it clearly in Matthew 5:38–42:

You have heard the law that says the punishment must match the injury: "An eye for an eye, and a tooth for a tooth." But I say, do not resist an evil person! If someone slaps you on the right cheek, offer the other cheek also. If you are sued in court and your shirt is taken from you, give your coat, too. If a soldier demands that you carry his gear for a mile, carry it two miles. Give to those who ask, and don't turn away from those who want to borrow.

One of the most powerful nuggets mined from these passages is the idea of going beyond obligation. Jesus is saying it's not enough to only do what you are obligated to do, the "don't." You must go above and beyond obligation—that's the "do." We need to do the "don't" without forgetting to do the "do!" (Are you following me?)

All the other religions stop at the first mile. Jesus teaches us to go the second. And stopping at obligation is one of the reasons Jesus called the Pharisees "blind guides" who were known to "strain out a gnat but swallow a camel" (Matthew 23:24). In other words, they would follow the rules only to fulfill their obligation, missing the more important things that brought the greatest reward!

Jesus really drives this point home in Matthew 5:20 (ESV) when He says, "For I tell you, unless your righteousness exceeds that of the scribes and Pharisees, you will never enter the kingdom of heaven." Notice the word *exceed*. It is the Greek word *perisseuó* and it means "to be over and above, to abound, to surpass." We could also say, go the extra mile.

Then in verses 21–49, Jesus really unpacks this concept. Each thought starts with Jesus saying: "You have heard . . .," then follows it with "but I tell you. . . ." What is He really telling us? Regardless of the subject, the message is the same: It's not enough to meet the obligation. You must also go the extra mile.

For example, in verses 21 and 22, Jesus says:

You have heard that our ancestors were told, "You must not murder. If you commit murder, you are subject to judgment." But I say, if you are even angry with someone, you are subject to judgment! If you call someone an idiot, you are in danger of being brought before the court. And if you curse someone, you are in danger of the fires of hell.

It's not enough to not murder someone—that's the obligation. You must also not insult them or curse them (we could insert complain or criticize here too). That's the extra mile. And He rounds out that section by saying in verse 44, "But I say, love your enemies! Pray for those who persecute you!" Jesus teaches that instead of giving them what they deserve, we go the extra mile and give what they don't deserve.

> ⑥
>
> *The reward—change!—is found in going the second mile.*

The reward goes beyond the satisfaction of carrying out your obligation. The reward—change!—is found in going the second mile. So, when Kim told me what she believed Holy Spirit was revealing to her, we discussed and felt like this is how it all connected.

When Jesus tells us to love our enemies (instead of hate) and pray for them (instead of curse), He is challenging us to look at things through a different lens. The invitation is to tackle the problem differently. The call is for a shift in focus.

We believe Holy Spirit showed us the key to deep and lasting change was not found in zipping our lips but in changing our focus. Instead of spending all our time and energy trying not to complain, biting our tongues, and smothering critical thoughts, we believe that we should reinvest our resources in changing perspectives—swapping ours for His.

Holy Spirit knew this would be a challenge for us. So, in His love for us, He gave us two powerful directives that, when applied, can change the trajectory of our lives.

STEP ONE: BE THANKFUL IN EVERYTHING

Step one is found in 1 Thessalonians 5:18: "Be thankful in all circumstances, for this is God's will for you who belong to Christ Jesus."

In this sentence, the word *thankful* is not an adjective. It's not a word used to describe or give more information about something. Instead, *thankful* is a verb—an action word. Holy Spirit is calling us to take action and be thankful—to act in thankfulness. His wisdom is directing us how to behave in all circumstances. This is the "do"—the extra mile.

Now, about that word *all*; it's the same Greek word we've looked at previously, *pas*. If you remember, it means all the individual pieces that make a whole and the whole itself. No exceptions.

For every circumstance and situation in our lives, we are instructed to act in thankfulness. To live in a mind-set that continually expresses gratitude. To have an attitude that appreciates and is grateful, regardless of what is happening. Thankful in the stretching, the uncomfortableness, the pain, the disappointment, the frustration, the heartbreak. When we are in those moments, feeling those negative feelings, experiencing those hard places, go the extra mile and choose to be thankful.

We had so many opportunities to implement this truth in our lives. For me (Kim) this was best seen during the recovery process from the Blight of '17. I am a somewhat finicky eater and I have an affinity for anything sweet. I don't just have a sweet tooth; I have a mouth full of sweet teeth. I will choose ice cream over real food any time. I can eat my weight in marshmallow peeps, and icing is the best food group in the world. (And yes, it's a group because there are different types, different flavors, and different colors.) I was devastated to learn our recovery program included clean—squeaky clean—eating. Absolutely no sugar. None whatsoever. Fruit was barely included. I almost threw in the towel and renounced my vow to not complain when I realized that we would mainly be eating grass. I was certain *this* would be the end of me because there was nothing on the list I'd want to eat. I was sure I would starve to death before I ever recovered.

Bill was quick to remind me, not just of the importance of making better food choices, but also of being thankful while I did it. And can I tell you, that was a true challenge. This segment of our recovery program was not just a week or even a month. It was indefinite. Not forever, but open-ended. I didn't even have a cutoff date to look forward to. I would think of having a birthday without cake and feel anger. I would imagine the holidays without my favorite foods and feel sad. Then I would feel ashamed for being traumatized by healthy eating.

Despite my angst, I knew that if I got tangled up in this food issue, I would derail my recovery. And I'm not referring to my physical recovery. I'm talking about my mental and spiritual recovery as I purposed to rewire my brain and demolish the stronghold of complaining. To be honest, it took me a bit to get a hold on this. I was angrier about this food thing than I realized. But I discovered that the more I expressed thankfulness in this area, the easier it became. It was a process and I had to be deliberate, but the more I chose gratitude, the more my attitude changed. And the more my attitude changed, the more grace I experienced. I believe His grace had always been available to me for this, but complaining had prevented me from seeing and connecting to it. As I practiced thankfulness, my heart was able to recognize His grace and sync with it as He freely poured it out, which made this aspect of the journey easier.

STEP TWO: BE THANKFUL FOR EVERYTHING

Step two is found in Ephesians 5:20: "And give thanks for everything to God the Father in the name of our Lord Jesus Christ."

Now, we know what you're thinking: It's hard enough to be thankful in difficult situations, but now He's asking us to be thankful *for* them? But listen to the intent of this wisdom. Holy Spirit is not asking you to be thankful for cancer, divorce, disaster, sickness, heartbreak, or mold and formaldehyde poisoning. Or any other painful thing for that matter. He's not asking you to appreciate the destructive tools of the enemy at work in your life. That's foolishness.

What He's asking is for you to look at the benefits of that situation in your life. Look beyond the emotional entanglements of the moment and see how Father God can take what was intended to harm you and use it for your good (Romans 8:28). Choose to see that the tools that the enemy meant to crush you with, God desires to use as a platform to propel you into your destiny (Genesis 50:20).

> ❦
>
> *Look beyond the emotional entanglements of the moment and see how Father God can take what was intended to harm you and use it for your good.*

Our oldest daughter, Gabrielle, was diagnosed with Type I Diabetes when she was five years old. At the time of this writing, we have lived with the struggles and pain of this disease for twenty-five years. We have run the gamut of emotions: shock, disappointment, anger, bitterness, resentment, panic, and denial. We have spiraled down the dark hole of fear and dread more times than we can count. None of these choices have benefited us emotionally, mentally, or spiritually. In fact, all the above made it more difficult for us to trust God and lean into Him in times of need.

However, when we chose thankfulness, everything changed. We chose to be thankful for the circumstances. We are *not* saying, "Thank you, God, for giving our daughter diabetes," because sickness and disease do not come from Father God. (He can't give you what He does not have.) But we are thankful for the opportunity to discover what we otherwise might have missed. We are saying thank you for circumstances that forced us to grow and mature. We are thankful for situations that revealed the heart of God in a way that we would have never seen it otherwise. We are grateful we've had a front-row seat to the supernatural and miraculous as we've seen Jesus take her hand time and time again. We are expressing appreciation because these conditions forced us to dig in deep, cling to Him, and learn to trust in ways that we did not know were possible.

And to be honest, we may not have done any of that without this situation. Because our circumstances forced our hand, we have gleaned so many truths, learned so many lessons, and discovered so much about Him that we are now radically different. There are things that were deposited in us that we would not exchange for anything. What the enemy intended to crush us with, God has used to increase us. Where the enemy purposed to limit us, God used it to expand us. Thankfulness turned our unpleasant journey into a triumphal procession. And it's not over. At the time of this writing, Gabrielle is in the middle of recovering from retina detachment in both eyes. To date, she's had nine eye surgeries and at least three more to come. But we are thankful for the opportunity to experience a miracle first hand and see God's Word come to life in her. As we eagerly anticipate her complete healing, we expect to learn even more.

The wisdom of Ephesians says be thankful for everything. Be thankful for the situation—the problem, the hardship, the burden, the loss, the pain, and the trials. Be thankful because those trying circumstances are opportunities to partner with Jesus and experience incredible revelation and lasting change. Those situations give you the chance to trust God and lean in like you didn't know you could. Those situations give you a front-row seat to a miracle you would otherwise miss.

Thankfulness, appreciation, and gratitude are the tools that help us shift our focus and gain His perspective. Without thankfulness, our eyes become focused and locked on our circumstances, keeping us trapped in a human perspective. And as we look at our circumstances and what we don't like about them, what we wish was different, what we want to change, the regrets we have, and the disappointments we experience, we become overwhelmed, frustrated, and weary. In our frustration and weariness, we begin to complain and criticize, and the results are always disastrous. The wrong focus creates the wrong perspective and causes us to quit, take matters into our own hands, or force change because our critical and complaining words put pressure on us, driving us to quick relief. We can never gain His perspective if our focus is wrong. We cannot look at our circumstances and God at the same time.

> *Thankfulness shifts our focus to Him and enables us to keep our eyes locked on Him.*

Thankfulness shifts our focus to Him and enables us to keep our eyes locked on Him. It allows us to exchange our perspectives for His and see things from His vantage point. To hear what He hears. To feel His heart on the situation. It enables us to journey with Him and go the extra mile.

And, thankfulness is a key component to the process of rewiring our brains. While the *don't* is important, the power is in the *do*. While it's important for us to not complain, criticize, argue, or be negative, it's more important for us to be thankful, grateful, and appreciative. It's more important that we go the extra mile and bless, encourage, and express appreciation and gratitude, because that's where the reward is—a changed heart.

It's not enough to withhold the complaint or criticism, we must also find something to be thankful for, something to appreciate, something to compliment. Don't just withhold the complaint; fill the void with thankfulness. For example, if your job is difficult, and your boss is demanding, be thankful that you have a job and a paycheck. When your spouse does *that* again, instead of complaining about it, appreciate their great qualities. Instead of criticizing elected officials for every decision they make, be thankful to live in a free country. Instead of complaining about your hooptie, be thankful you aren't walking everywhere. Instead of whining about your circumstances, be thankful that God causes everything to work together for the good of those who love Him and are called according to His purpose (Romans 8:28)!

Do you get the idea? From the macro to the micro, replace the complaint with gratitude. Trade what *you* see for what *He* sees. We're not suggesting that you view the world through rose-colored glasses. This is not about pretending. This is about seeing what He sees and saying what He says. There is always something to appreciate about every person and every situation—even if there's just one thing.

This reminds me (Kim) of a story my mom told me. When she was young, she had a neighbor who was a drunk. At all hours of the day and night, they would hear this man creating a ruckus. He was loud, obnoxious, and rude. But he had a habit of whistling, and he could do it quite well. One day, she overheard her parents discussing the neighbor. Her dad was complaining about the problems he created. And in the middle of those complaints, she heard her mother say, "But he sure can whistle."

> ⑥
> *Trade what* you *see for what* He *sees.*

My grandma got it. She found the one thing. While there didn't seem to be anything to appreciate about this man, she chose to find the one thing to compliment and she talked about that. She appreciated his talent instead of criticizing his weakness. I imagine she called him "the whistler" instead of "the drunk."

So, whatever your circumstances are, find at least one thing and focus on it. Appreciate it. Talk about it. Think on it. And if you can't seem to find it, ask Holy Spirit what it is. He has a bird's eye view and can see what you can't. Ask Him to reveal what is true, honorable, right, pure, lovely, and admirable, and then think on those things (Philippians 4:8).

FINDING ABUNDANT JOY

We've certainly had our share of doctor visits, lab work, and testing as we journeyed to regain our health. Regardless of the symptoms, the root cause of the imbalance or abnormality was always the same: toxicity due to long-term mold and formaldehyde exposure. As doctors worked with us to resolve issues, they prescribed various treatments, diet changes, supplements, and medications, all intended to support our bodies during recovery. As these things worked together, they rooted out the toxicity, restored health, and improved our lives.

This is precisely what happens when we address spiritual and soul (mind, will, and emotion) symptoms with Jesus. Regardless of the symptoms being addressed, the root cause of our issues is always the same: long-term exposure to sin. As Jesus works in our lives to help us step into freedom and experience the abundant life He died to give us, He prescribes change with strong doses of truth, both intended to help support our souls during recovery. As we partner with Him, sin is rooted out, wholeness is restored, and our lives improve.

One of the greatest benefits of His work in our lives is the growth of abundant joy.

Joy is such a wonderful word; its very sound evokes positive emotion. It paints pictures of ecstatic exuberance twirling in absolute delight. It's something we all want, but it appears to be elusive, only available to the few who are able to find it. Even fewer seem to have the ability to hang on to it.

But joy seems difficult to obtain because the word *joy* is misused and misunderstood. To clarify, we'll start by telling you what joy is not. Joy is not happiness or being happy. Happiness is an emotion—and a fickle one at that. The root of the word *happiness* is *hap*, which means "chance, luck, or circumstances." The basis of happiness is circumstantial, which is why it's an emotion. Happiness is based upon life going the way we want it to go and the feeling we experience when it does. Happiness is a good feeling based upon good circumstances.

There's not anything wrong with being happy. We want to be happy. God wants us to experience happiness. But unfortunately, happiness is fleeting and elusive because it is based on ever-changing circumstances. We often have events, days, or seasons when we don't experience happiness because our circumstances are not ideal, not what we planned, or not what we wanted—all of which create opportunities to complain and criticize.

> *Joy is much deeper than emotion. . . Joy is having an attitude that celebrates God's character.*

However, joy is a completely different concept. Joy has nothing to do with our emotions or how we feel and everything to do with what we know and believe. Joy is much deeper than emotion, more firm and secure because joy is an attitude or a mind-set. An attitude is the habitual, typical, and normal thought process that determines how you will interpret and respond to situations. In other words, your attitude is the lens through which you see life. It governs your words and actions.

Joy is having an attitude that celebrates God's character. It is not contingent upon ever-changing circumstances but is anchored in the never-changing nature of our perfect God. Joy refuses to be influenced by the negative situations that come and go, and it chooses to anchor itself in God's goodness and faithfulness. Joy is convinced that God is willing to help us, and it trusts His ability to do the impossible. Joy is knowing God and believing He will do what He promised. Joy is a solid and firm confidence in God.

When we intimately know God—have more than mere information about Him, but actually experience and live in His heart—we are able to trust Him. In this place of trust, our confidence in Him grows. From this confidence, joy erupts from our souls. It doesn't mean that we will always be happy, bubbly, and thrilled. It doesn't mean we will be blind to difficult situations or relationships, but it does mean that we will experience peace and have rest in our souls as we journey through these situations. Joy is relief from the mental strain of fear, worry, and anxiety.

When we are certain of God's goodness, fear, worry, and anxiety have no place to land in our hearts and minds because they are full of joy—confidence in God. There is no need to stress or panic. There is no need to vent or emotionally vomit on anyone. Joy looks at the situation, connects the problem with God's promise of provision, and gives birth to both peace and hope.

> *Joy is relief from the mental strain of fear, worry, and anxiety.*

Biblical peace is satisfaction, fullness, rest, quiet, calm, tranquility, and stillness of the spirit and soul, and it is based upon the presence of God. It is not contingent upon our emotions or external conditions. It is not fragile but possesses the full strength and authority of God. As we celebrate the character of God, His presence fills our souls and blankets us with peace that passes all understanding. We have unexplainable tranquility as situations that merit grumbling swirl chaotically around us. While our circumstances say we should be frustrated, irritated, or angry, God's presence calms our souls as we trust Him to help us navigate through rough waters.

Biblical hope is the confident expectation that God is everything He said He is and will do everything He said He would do. Therefore, we anticipate goodness to come from every difficulty, trial, and obstacle. Biblical hope is not crossing its fingers with a furrowed brow. Biblical hope is rooted in the reality that Jesus Christ is the same yesterday, today, and forever (Hebrews 13:8). When we choose joy, unending hope will follow.

We personally know this to be true because this is exactly what we experienced during the Blight of '17. Refusing to complain created a silence in our minds and our conversations. We chose to fill the silence with confident declarations of God's goodness and faithfulness. We did not live in denial, nor did we bury our heads in the sand. We acknowledged the difficulties we were experiencing, but we always followed those acknowledgements with "but God…" We choose to acknowledge God's goodness and faithfulness more than the difficulties. We are not saying we did it perfectly; we did have our moments of frustration, despair, and disappointment. However, when we chose to fix our eyes on the character of God and celebrate Him in the middle of difficulties, without fail we found joy surge through our souls, and peace and hope overwhelmed us. Nothing changed around us, but everything changed within us.

DAVID FOUND ABUNDANT JOY

We think David must have latched on to this reality because this is how he seemed to live his life. We see the evidence of joy in David's life in 1 Samuel 30. During this time, David, his men, and their families were living in Philistine territory because King Saul and his army were pursuing David to kill him (chapter 27). David and his men had gone out to fight with the Philistine army, leaving their wives and children at home. When they returned, they discovered the Amalekites had pillaged their compound, burning it to the ground, taking all the women and children captive. They arrived in Ziglag to find it a deserted ruin. First Samuel 30:4–6 tells us how these events unfolded:

> When David and his men saw the ruins and realized what had happened to their families, they wept until they could weep no more. David's two wives, Ahinoam from Jezreel and Abigail, the widow of Nabal from Carmel, were among those captured. David was now in great danger because all his men were very bitter about losing their sons and daughters, and they began to talk of stoning him. But David found strength in the Lord his God.

There's no denying, there was plenty of room for fear, panic, and anger. These emotions easily gave way to complaining, criticizing, and arguing. We see this quickly unfold in the lives of David's men. This cocktail of toxicity created a plan for murder. But look at David's attitude. He did not focus on the tragic circumstances. He didn't even focus on calming his men down or saving his own neck. David's response to this tragedy and the fear and anger brewing among the men was to strengthen himself. He did not accomplish this through positive self-talk by saying things like, "Ok, buddy, you can do this. You can figure this out. You're the giant-killer! You can handle this." Instead he strengthened himself with trust in God.

David looked at God. He turned his attention away from his emotions and circumstances and focused on God's goodness and faithfulness. He recounted all the times God had promised and provided. He remembered God's majesty, strength, and power. He focused on God's character and nature.

You can also see this attitude as he journaled his conversations with God in the Psalms. He wrote in Psalm 28:7: "The Lord is my strength and shield. I trust him with all my heart. He helps me, and my heart is filled with joy. I burst out in songs of thanksgiving." In Psalm 16:8–9 (TPT) he says: "Because you are close to me and always available, my confidence will never be shaken, for I experience your wrap-around presence every moment. My heart and soul explode with joy—full of glory! Even my body will rest confident and secure."

One of the things we noticed from David's writings is that joy was a choice he made. He chose to trust in God. He chose to put his confidence in God. It was a decision he made. Unlike happiness, joy is not a feeling that comes because everything is going pleasantly in our lives. Instead, joy is the result of a choice we make. We choose whether or not we will trust God. We choose whether or not we will rest in Him. We choose whether or not we will believe His promises and the truth of

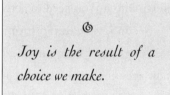

Joy is the result of a choice we make.

the Word. And when we choose to have confidence in God and trust Him, that joyful attitude is developed and nurtured. As joy grows, peace and hope overflow into our emotions, producing satisfaction and contentment, curbing grief or sadness, and eliminating stress and anxiety. Joy does not wait for everything to fall into place first. Joy chooses to trust that God will lead us into His perfect plan and rests in that fact. Joy does not wait for circumstances and relationships to be problem-free before it celebrates. Joy chooses to believe God's goodness and celebrates His provision in advance.

That's why James 1:2 says when troubles of any kind come your way, you can consider it an opportunity for great joy. Instead of grumbling, consider this an opportunity to exercise great confidence in the perfect goodness and faithfulness of God before anything changes. Even if nothing ever changes. This is the key to not only surviving, but thriving in difficulties and painful circumstances!

FINDING JOY

We will admit, this is not easy. We often have to lean on Holy Spirit for His strength and power to choose the attitude of joy. But here are some things we've learned that have helped and encouraged us on this journey.

First, know that joy is already inside you. To us, this is the best news! We don't have to earn it or search for it; it's living inside us! Joy is a fruit of the Spirit (Galatians 5:22–23). It is a by-product of Holy Spirit. Wherever He is, you will find joy—absolute, unwavering confidence in God. When you stepped into relationship with Father God through Jesus Christ, Holy Spirit moved into you, spirit, soul, and body. When He moved in, He brought all that He is and all that He has with Him. So, the fullness of God lives in you, and that includes joy. You already have joy—all the joy that exists. You just need to tap into it. You need to activate it.

Second, we can tap into joy by reading the Bible. Psalm 19:8 (TPT) tells us: "His teachings make us joyful and radiate his light; his precepts are so pure! His commands, how they challenge us to keep close to his heart! The revelation-light of his word makes my spirit shine radiant." Reading the Bible connects us to the joy within because it reveals the nature and character of God. Our confidence soars as we see His goodness, kindness, and love. Our trust increases as we see Him faithfully providing for His people. Our belief is strengthened as we see His might, authority, and power on display. We can't help but trust when we read testimony after testimony of His greatness!

Third, we connect to joy by meditating on His promises. Psalm 119:162 (TPT) says, "Your promises are the source of my bubbling joy; the revelation of your word thrills me like one who has discovered hidden treasure." The Bible contains thousands of promises.

They are explicit declarations made by God for us that we can fully rely on. Whatever you need, God has a promise for you. If you will spend time meditating on the promises of God, filling your thoughts with His commitments to you, and memorizing them, then your confidence in Him will grow exponentially and joy will bubble over.

> ⑥
> *Whatever you need, God has a promise for you.*

Finally, we activate joy as we rejoice. While meditation is an inward action focusing on God's character, rejoicing is the outward demonstration of what's going on in our hearts. To rejoice is to be glad and take delight in who God is, what He has done, and what He is doing, as it anticipates what He will do. In wisdom, Philippians 4:4 (AMP) encourages us to, "Rejoice in the Lord always [delight, take pleasure in Him]; again I will say, rejoice!" We really like the way it's worded in *The Message*: "Celebrate God all day, every day. I mean, revel [take great pleasure or delight, make merry, indulge in boisterous festivities] in him!" When we actively celebrate God, verbally declaring the beauty of His perfect nature and righteous character, regardless of our circumstances or feelings, joy explodes in our lives!

In this process of healing for our souls, joy is both the antidote and inoculation for complaining and criticism. As we choose to cultivate the habitual thought process that God is more than enough for any problem we face and let that attitude shape our words and actions, there is no room for complaining or critical thoughts and words. Not only will this choice root out any toxicity that is present, but it will prevent any more from developing. Joy really is the cure for complaining and criticism.

PAUL FOUND ABUNDANT JOY

One last thought as we close this chapter. We encourage you to read the book of Philippians, also known as "the book of joy." Through the inspiration of Holy Spirit, Paul wrote the book of Philippians as a letter to the church of Philippi while he was imprisoned in Rome. Throughout the book, Paul expressed his great joy. Being in prison, Paul could have grumbled, been angry, or grown bitter. Instead, he chose gratitude and trusted God.

While he probably would have chosen to freely share the gospel outside the confines of a prison cell, he still managed to reach his church plants by writing letters and sending messages to them through couriers. The results of his choice to remain joyful are that he not only ministered to those who received the letters, but in the centuries since he died he has made an eternal impact upon millions as he urged every reader to be joyful and rejoice because he knew how beneficial it had been to him. He knew how powerful rejoicing is.

As he closed out the letter, he shared the secret of dealing with complaint-worthy circumstances: "I know how to live on almost nothing or with everything. I have learned the secret of living in every situation, whether it is with a full stomach or empty, with plenty or little. For I can do everything through Christ, who gives me strength" (Philippians 4:12–13). Paul was able to live in every situation through Christ who enabled, empowered, and infused him with inner strength. Paul was able to trust God for this strength because he knew God's character and could trust Him.

Before you move on, take some time to ask yourself the questions: What do I really believe about God? Do I know His character? Am I intimately acquainted with His nature? This will go a long way in helping you connect with and live in abundant joy.

Part**Two**

The History of Complaining

8

THERE'S A SNAKE IN THE ROOTS

We've already had a little science lesson. Now, let's take a look at history. Let's go back to the beginning and look at the earliest records of complaining to see what we can learn from these events.

Complaining is not a modern-day phenomenon. Humans have a long, sordid history of complaining. From the beginning of time, complaining has been a part of the human experience, wreaking havoc and destruction. You would think by now we would have learned from the mistakes of history and eradicated complaining as efficiently as we've eliminated smallpox. In light of history, you'd think we would view criticizing as as deadly as the black plague and take precautions to avoid it at all cost. Perhaps if we renamed "complaining" to be called "the black plague" it would change our perspective.

Maybe that's been our problem. Maybe we aren't looking at complaining and all its various forms as deadly and contagious. Maybe we've normalized it and determined it's just how things are. Maybe we've failed to connect the dots, linking complaining to its lethal consequences. Maybe we've failed to link complaining to its original source.

We'll begin where it all started, in the Garden. Genesis 3:1–13 says:

The serpent was the shrewdest of all the wild animals the LORD God had made. One day he asked the woman, "Did God really say you must not eat the fruit from any of the trees in the garden?"

"Of course, we may eat fruit from the trees in the garden," the woman replied. "It's only the fruit from the tree in the middle of the garden that we are not allowed to eat. God said, 'You must not eat it or even touch it; if you do, you will die.'"

"You won't die!" the serpent replied to the woman. "God knows that your eyes will be opened as soon as you eat it, and you will be like God, knowing both good and evil."

The woman was convinced. She saw that the tree was beautiful and its fruit looked delicious, and she wanted the wisdom it would give her. So she took some of the fruit and ate it. Then she gave some to her husband, who was with her, and he ate it, too. At that moment their eyes were opened, and they suddenly felt shame at their nakedness. So they sewed fig leaves together to cover themselves.

When the cool evening breezes were blowing, the man and his wife heard the LORD God walking about in the garden. So they hid from the LORD God among the trees. Then the LORD God called to the man, "Where are you?"

He replied, "I heard you walking in the garden, so I hid. I was afraid because I was naked."

"Who told you that you were naked?" the LORD God asked. "Have you eaten from the tree whose fruit I commanded you not to eat?"

The man replied, "It was the woman you gave me who gave me the fruit, and I ate it."

Then the LORD God asked the woman, "What have you done?"

"The serpent deceived me," she replied. "That's why I ate it."

There it is. Right there in verse one, the record of the first complaint and criticism ever made on Earth. It's subtle. It's sly. But it's there.

While there's no documentation to support our theory, we think this was one of many conversations held between Eve and the serpent. We have this notion because there's no indication that she is surprised by his approach or uncomfortable with his presence. She seems to willingly participate in the conversation. She seems to be attentive and responsive to what he has to say. She even considers his words to be credible. It appears as though they have enough history between them that she doesn't even question his logic and is easily and quickly convinced.

But what seems to be their normal, laidback conversation takes a twist this time and ends up being the culmination of a diabolical coup. Even though satan's[11] approach to Eve was casual, subtle, and familiar, he came to incite a riot. Create an uprising. Provoke rebellion. The question he asked may have seemed innocent enough, but the intent was pure evil. The motive was maleficent. With accurately aimed arrows—he's been using those "fiery darts" for a long time—he set Eve's mind ablaze with a subtle complaint against God. Maybe her mind caught fire so quickly and easily because all along he had been strategically placing kindling in just the right places. Maybe?

Appearing so sincere, he asked her, "Did God really say you must not eat the fruit from any of the trees in the garden?" Don't be fooled; he was not curious. Instead, he was baiting her with a hissed murmur against God disguised as a question. Gingerly casting an accusation, he was stirring the waters of discontent with a sly but intentional innuendo against God.

> *Instead, he was baiting her with a hissed murmur against God disguised as a question.*

Eve's response is telling. She said, "Of course we may eat fruit from the trees in the garden. It's only the fruit from the tree in the middle of the garden that we are not allowed to eat. God said, 'You must not eat it or even touch it; if you do, you will die'" (vv. 2–3).

Now, it sounds like Eve was giving the right response; however, her memory had become a bit fuzzy regarding what God really said. In Genesis 2:16–17 God gave clear instructions concerning the trees and their fruit when He said, "You may freely eat the fruit of every tree in the garden—except the tree of the knowledge of good and evil." Her slightly inaccurate response to the serpent indicated she had taken the bait, because she added the "or even touch it" part. Can you hear the undertone of her words as she hinted that God was too controlling? Her exaggeration leaned toward the critical.

She also failed to specify which tree in the middle of the garden. According to Genesis 2:9, there were two trees in the center of the garden: "In the middle of the garden he placed the tree of life and the tree of the knowledge of good and evil." Already her perception was skewed as she said nothing of the amazing Tree of Life, from which they could eat *freely*.

Sensing she had nibbled on his line, the serpent set the hook. If verse one was subtle, verses four and five are blatant as he brazenly declared: "You won't die! God knows that your eyes will be opened as soon as you eat it, and you will be like God, knowing both good and evil." This is the second complaint recorded in history. With this lie, the serpent criticized God, suggesting that He has been holding out on Eve. The serpent implied there was more to be had, there were things that she was unaware of. Things she was missing out on. The criticism was that God was not as good as He appeared to be because He put limits and restrictions on Eve's freedom. Listen carefully, and you'll hear the underlying timbre of anger and resentment (the tenor of criticism) in his objection. In essence, he was saying: "Sounds to me like God really doesn't want you to have everything, Eve. He doesn't want you to be happy. Or satisfied. Content or fulfilled. It sounds like God wants you to go without."

Complaints and criticism are nasty tentacles of pride.

And that's when Eve took the bait—hook, line, and sinker. Genesis 3:6 tells us, "The woman was convinced. She saw that the tree was beautiful and its fruit looked delicious, and she wanted the wisdom it would give her. So she took some of the fruit and ate it." With a quick flick of his tongue, the serpent reeled her in with a lie baited with complaint and criticism.

And why wouldn't he fish with that bait? Complaints and criticism had always been his modus operandi. Ezekiel 28:12–18 and Isaiah 14:12–14 both tell the saga of lucifer, one of Heaven's arch angels. The blameless model of perfection, lucifer orchestrated adoration and honor to Father God as he led all of Heaven in worship. At some point, pride erupted in lucifer's heart when he determined God was no longer worthy of all this praise and admiration. In that moment, he set out to place himself above Father God and establish himself as a deity—as one above God.

Complaints and criticisms are nasty tentacles of pride. Once you've determined you are better, superior, or deserve more than another, complaints and criticisms naturally follow. While the Bible does not explicitly say this, we believe that lucifer's admiration of God soured. He critically evaluated God and concluded that he, himself, was every bit as worthy of Heaven's applause as God was. As conceit and arrogance stirred in his heart, he began to share these critical thoughts with the hosts of Heaven, complaining about God's character, worth, leadership, and prominence.

The moment pride erupted in lucifer's heart, God instantly dealt with his sin and treason. Revelation 12:3–4 gives us insight into this event: "Then I witnessed in heaven another significant event. I saw a large red dragon with seven heads and ten horns, with seven crowns on his heads. His tail swept away one-third of the stars in the sky, and he threw them to the earth."

Did you see that? Did you see how lucifer's tail swept away one-third of the hosts of Heaven and threw them to the Earth. His tail. His "tale." The fictitious narrative laced with complaints and criticisms about and against God. With his complaining words, lucifer's infectious tale poisoned the minds of one-third of Heaven's angels, turning them away from the heart of God. The effect of this poison was division. An eternal rift. An explosive rupture that created a permanent gulf.

Complaining and criticism were so effective in creating alliances in Heaven and dividing Father God from His creation, that lucifer implemented the same tactics on Earth. This was his weapon of choice in seducing Eve.

But even though lucifer—satan, the great dragon, the serpent—was the mastermind of this diabolical plan to set Eve up for failure, Eve was not without fault. Yes, he deceived her. Yes, he took advantage of her. Yes, he manipulated her. Yes, he lied. But he would never have caught her unaware if she had consulted with Father God on her conversations with the serpent. She could have talked to God about the serpent as He came to enjoy an evening walk with them each day, and He would have warned her about the enemy. He would have exposed the serpent for the conniving traitor he really was. He would have told her everything she needed to know. He would have taught her how to effectively deal with this foul creature disguised as a snake.

Apart from Father God, Eve drew her own conclusions about the serpent. Without any insight, facts, or truth, she formed her own opinions. (See how dangerous that can be?!) Without any understanding or history of the creature or his wicked intentions, she determined this serpent was like every other animal in the Garden. In her thinking, chats with the serpent were just as normal and interesting as conversations with any other animal. Her independent assumptions and opinions caused her to befriend the enemy of God. The enemy of humanity. And she opened the door for the enemy to have access to the human race. It all started with complaints and criticism. That is sobering.

One last thought before we close out this chapter. Did you notice how subtle the serpent's tactics are with Eve? We know he didn't come to her announcing his true identity. Of course, he did not reveal his intentions to deceive her, lie to her, or start a rebellion against God. What if he had said, "Hello, Eve, my name is lucifer and I attempted to overthrow God—the One Who handcrafted you and loves you. The One you love. Don't mind the fact that my snake disguise is for the purpose of deceiving you, or that my plan is to lie to you through false complaints and accusations against Him. Listen carefully and agree with me." That's just silly. The enemy never operates like that.

Instead, he came quietly, softly, blending in. In casual, easy conversation with her over the course of time, he allowed her to become comfortable with him until he found a place of familiarity and trust; he built credibility with her. We watch as he was patient to bide his time until he knew his words carried weight with her. In fact, he was so discreet and subtle that she never saw it coming. Before she knew what happened, she had been sucked into a vortex so great that she could not find her way out.

And here we are today, still dealing with implications of this seemingly innocent conversation. Oh-so-subtle complaints and criticisms from him against God continue to cause destruction today. We know his tactics, language, and character have not changed. The enemy—lucifer, the serpent, the devil, the great dragon—is the source of all complaining, and he is constantly trying to incite a riot, drum up rebellion, and create division.

There is so much to learn from history! In the next chapter, we'll look at other historical events that show the devastation of complaints and criticism. But before we get there, take some time to reflect on this history lesson. This one is too important to just breeze over.

9

THE LONG WAY HOME

In his 1905 book series *The Life of Reason: The Phases of Human Progress,* George Santayana famously said: "Those who cannot remember the past are condemned to repeat it."[12] We agree with that, but we like this modified version often attributed to Winston Churchill even better: "Those who fail to learn from the past are doomed to repeat it." No truer words have ever been spoken. You might know about the past or have information regarding a past event, but if you didn't learn from it, more than likely you will repeat it. We think the previous chapter proves this point.

In the Christian world, we often look at the children of Abraham and are astounded at their foolishness in turning a journey that should have taken days into one that took decades—forty years to be exact. As believers, we are shocked at their repeated rejection of God as they embraced false gods. We look at the vicious cycle they lived in and shake our heads, wondering how they could have been so blind. Unfortunately, many of us are repeating their history and living in the same vicious cycle because we view these historical events as mere stories and not invaluable truths from which we should learn.

With that in mind, let's look at another snapshot from history.

One of the most incredible events in all of human history is the deliverance of the children of Israel from the Egyptians. This magnificent account is found in the second book of the Old Testament, Exodus, as well as in portions of Numbers and Deuteronomy. For approximately four hundred years, the sons and daughters of Abraham, whom we'll call "the children of Israel," "Israelites," or "the Hebrews," had been held captive by a succession of Pharaohs who conscripted them into slavery, forcing them to build the cities of Egypt. The nation of Egypt was fueled by the slave labor of the Hebrews. The tyranny was so ruthless and oppressive that the Hebrews groaned under the burden of slavery and cried out to God for help. Father God heard their cries for deliverance and moved on their behalf.

That's when He sent Moses to liberate them from slavery. As God's spokesman, Moses approached Pharaoh and requested that the Hebrews be released to journey into the desert to worship God. Pharaoh scoffed at the idea and responded in brutality by increasing the demands of slavery upon the Hebrews. That's when God turned up the heat.

God's response to Pharaoh's cruelty was a glorious display of His power and might. Each time Moses requested the release of the Hebrews, Pharaoh arrogantly refused. And for each refusal, God responded with a plague. Not just any plague, but ten plagues that were deliberate insults to Egyptian gods. As each plague swept through Egypt, God was systematically dismantling the power of these false gods as He showed His preeminence over them. In an unprecedented display of authority and supremacy, God revealed to Egypt that He alone is the One True Living God. He simultaneously revealed to the Hebrews that He was superior, not only to the Egyptian gods, but to the pharaoh himself. They could sever any alliances they may have had with those pagan deities.

Father God also revealed His faithfulness to the Hebrews as He shielded them from seven of the ten calamities. While all of Egypt was being pummeled by supernatural acts, the area of Goshen where the Hebrews lived was spared. They were completely unaffected by most of the judgements that tore through Egypt. This revealed to the Hebrews God's commitment to care for and protect them.

Then, when Pharaoh finally relented and allowed the Hebrews to leave, God blessed them with the wealth of Egypt. He instructed them to ask the Egyptians for clothing and articles of silver and gold. They obeyed, and God gave them divine favor with the Egyptians; they granted the Hebrews anything and everything they asked for. In essence, they stripped Egypt of its wealth, walking out of slavery with the treasure of their oppressors on their backs, lining their pockets and filling their bags as they took great flocks and herds of livestock with them. This retribution for four hundred years of slavery revealed to the Hebrews that not only was God just, but He was also their provider and would lavishly supply every need.

As they walked out of Egypt, Father God gave them a physical manifestation of His presence, leading them through the desert with a pillar of cloud by day and a pillar of fire by night. The pillar of cloud escorted them as they traveled during the day, sheltering them from the intense desert heat. By night, the pillar of fire covered them, giving them light and comfort in the deep darkness of the desert nights and warmth in the frigid desert temperatures. This revealed to the Hebrews that they were never alone; Father God was with them. The pillars were a display of His faithfulness as He led them, proving that He was caring and providing for them.

Pharaoh, of course, regretted his decision to let the Hebrews go. He led the Egyptian army in pursuit of the Hebrews to bring them back to enslavement in Egypt. As the Egyptians pressed the Hebrews to the shores of the Red Sea, God miraculously parted the waters and ushered His people through on dry ground to the other side. Somewhere between one and 2.5 million Hebrews crossed through to safety that day, but when the Egyptian army chased them into the path God created, He released the waters and the sea swallowed them whole. In one fell swoop, their enemies were annihilated. Their freedom was secured. Their deliverance was finalized. In this magnificent act, God demonstrated His ability to deliver and fight for Israel.

> *From the beginning to the end, God marvelously displayed His faithfulness, willingness, and ability to deliver, protect, provide, and secure them.*

From the beginning to the end, God marvelously displayed His faithfulness, willingness, and ability to deliver, protect, provide, and secure them. There wasn't a need He did not meet. There wasn't a situation He could not or did not handle. Miracle after miracle continuously revealed His love, devotion, and commitment to Israel. You would think that gratitude and appreciation would pour from their hearts and celebration and praise would consume them. But that's not what we hear the Hebrews saying. Listen to their words. Observe their tone. Highlight and note what you notice:

- Exodus 14:10–12: "As Pharaoh approached, the people of Israel looked up and panicked when they saw the Egyptians overtaking them. They cried out to the Lord, and they said to Moses, "Why did you bring us out here to die in the wilderness? Weren't there enough graves for us in Egypt? What have you done to us? Why did you make us leave Egypt? Didn't we tell you this would happen while we were still in Egypt? We said, 'Leave us alone! Let us be slaves to the Egyptians. It's better to be a slave in Egypt than a corpse in the wilderness!'"

- Exodus 15:24: "Then the people complained and turned against Moses. 'What are we going to drink?' they demanded."

- Exodus 16:2–3: "There, too, the whole community of Israel complained about Moses and Aaron. 'If only the LORD had killed us back in Egypt,' they moaned. 'There we sat around pots filled with meat and ate all the bread we wanted. But now you have brought us into this wilderness to starve us all to death.'"

- Exodus 17:2: "So once more the people complained against Moses. 'Give us water to drink!' they demanded. 'Quiet!' Moses replied. 'Why are you complaining against me? And why are you testing the LORD?'"

- Numbers 14:2: "Their voices rose in a great chorus of protest against Moses and Aaron. 'If only we had died in Egypt, or even here in the wilderness!' they complained."

- Numbers 21:5: "And they began to speak against God and Moses. 'Why have you brought us out of Egypt to die here in the wilderness?' they complained. 'There is nothing to eat here and nothing to drink. And we hate this horrible manna!'"

Do you hear it? Complaint after complaint. You'll find even more complaints listed in Numbers 11 as they grumbled and whined about the difficulties of living in the desert, the manna God provided, and the lack of meat. They were not satisfied and pined for the food of Egypt (the food of slavery). And in chapter 12, Miriam and Aaron criticized Moses, his leadership, and his choice for a wife.

Then, in chapter 13, we read that the Hebrews are standing on the precipice of the Promised Land, preparing to embark into a country of their own. It is the culmination of Exodus 3:17 when God told Moses: "I have promised to rescue you from your oppression in Egypt. I will lead you to a land flowing with milk and honey." It's not just any land, it's the Promised Land, gushing with sweet provision. It's what they've all been waiting for. So, they sent twelve spies in to scope out the terrain. When the spies returned, ten of them complained about what they saw. Their complaints spread like wildfire, inciting the entire community to rebel. Sound familiar?!

Chapter 14 tells the whole ugly story:

Then the whole community began weeping aloud, and they cried all night. Their voices rose in a great chorus of protest against Moses and Aaron. "If only we had died in Egypt, or even here in the wilderness!" they complained. "Why is the LORD taking us to this country only to have us die in battle? Our wives and our little ones will be carried off as plunder! Wouldn't it be better for us to return to Egypt?" Then they plotted among themselves, "Let's choose a new leader and go back to Egypt!" (vv. 1–4)

And it went downhill from there. There was talk of stoning the two spies who did not complain. God's anger was stirred. Moses interceded for the Hebrews. And it ended with this declaration from God in Numbers 14:26–29:

Then the LORD said to Moses and Aaron, "How long must I put up with this wicked community and its complaints about me? Yes, I have heard the complaints the Israelites are making against me. Now tell them this: 'As surely as I live, declares the LORD, I will do to you the very things I heard you say. You will all drop dead in this wilderness! Because you complained against me, every one of you who is twenty years old or older and was included in the registration will die.'"

Another version of this is also recorded in Deuteronomy 1:26–36:

But you rebelled against the command of the LORD your God and refused to go in. You complained in your tents and said, "The LORD must hate us. That's why he has brought us here from Egypt—to hand us over to the Amorites to be slaughtered. Where can we go? Our brothers have demoralized us with their report. They tell us, 'The people of the land are taller and more powerful than we are, and their towns are large, with walls rising high into the sky! We even saw giants there—the descendants of Anak!'"

But I said to you, "Don't be shocked or afraid of them! The LORD your God is going ahead of you. He will fight for you, just as you saw him do in Egypt. And you saw how the LORD your God cared for you all along the way as you traveled through the wilderness, just as a father cares for his child. Now he has brought you to this place."

But even after all he did, you refused to trust the LORD your God, who goes before you looking for the best places to camp, guiding you with a pillar of fire by night and a pillar of cloud by day.

When the LORD heard your complaining, he became very angry. So he solemnly swore, "Not one of you from this wicked generation will live to see the good land I swore to give your ancestors, except Caleb son of Jephunneh."

The Hebrews were not allowed to enter the Promised Land—not because they had worshiped a golden calf (recorded in Exodus 32), didn't trust God, had no faith, or were terrified, but because they complained. Yes, they built and worshiped a golden calf with the treasures of Egypt God had given them. Yes, they did not trust God. Yes, they had no faith. Yes, they were terrified. But all those things were the results of complaining.

Complaining and criticizing set them up for failure because it turned their eyes from the promise and caused them to focus on the problem. It was as if they had giant binoculars that zoomed in on every obstacle that came their way. Their complaints magnified the problem so they could no longer see the magnitude of God. Complaining blinded them from seeing what God had already done, what He was doing in the moment, and what He would do for them in the future. Complaining kept them from trusting, smothering their faith and keeping them in fear. Complaining kept them from the promise—a land of their own, flowing with sweet provision.

Complaining and criticizing set them up for failure because it turned their eyes from the promise and caused them to focus on the problem.

For the record, we are not implying that God will deal with us as He did the Hebrews when they complained. While God never changes, how He interacts with humanity has changed since the cross. But even today, complaining blinds us from the reality of God's goodness and it is not okay with God. God does not view complaining as a minor infraction; He views complaining as evil. It's a much bigger deal than we think.

There are consequences to complaining. For the Israelites, the consequences of complaining and criticism was delay. God never left them and faithfully cared for them. Evidence of His care and provision is seen as He fed them (Exodus 16:35) and their clothes and shoes never wore out (Deuteronomy 29:5–6). However, they wandered in the desert for forty years before they could enter the Promised Land.

This is a powerful lesson from history. Unless we learn from their past, we will be doomed to repeat their mistakes of missing the goodness of God. With that in mind, you may want to take some time to let this one soak in before you jump into the next chapter. Consider the possibility that complaining and criticism could be keeping you from connecting to a promise of God and hindering you from stepping into a season flowing with sweet provision.

10

THE PITFALL OF UNFORGIVENESS

Hindsight is twenty-twenty. That's the beauty of history. It affords us the opportunity to see things from a clear vantage point so that we can learn valuable lessons and avoid pitfalls. There are many valuable lessons to be learned in the history of Michal, the first wife of David. You can find her complete story woven through 1 and 2 Samuel, so we'll just cover the highlights here.

Even though she was the daughter of King Saul, life for Michal had not always been easy. She had married the love of her life, David the giant-killer, only to find her marriage was orchestrated by her father for the sole purpose of killing him (1 Samuel 18:20–21). In order to spare his life, she warned David of her father's murderous plot against him and helped him flee. Their plan for a successful escape involved David leaving her behind (1 Samuel 19:11–18). David knew it would never be safe to return for Michal or be any-where near Saul, so for fourteen years they were apart as he lived the life of a fugitive, constantly on the move, hiding from Saul and his army.

In an attempt to break all ties with David and further insult him, Saul gave Michal to another man in marriage (1 Samuel 25:44). It seemed as if she would forever be separated from the love of her life. The Bible doesn't say how long she was married to Phalti, but we speculate that it was long enough for her heart to heal and love to blossom. When Saul died and David ascended to the throne of Israel, he demanded that his wife be returned to him. As Michal was escorted away form Phalti, he followed, weeping with heartbroken sorrow (2 Samuel 3:13–15). We can assume Michal had been a loving and honorable wife to him.

Once she arrived in David's home, she discovered that David had taken on six additional wives and had children with them during their separation. Surely this was salt in the very deep wound of Michal's abused heart. Imagine her resentment at being forced to leave Phalti, the husband who loved and cherished her, to return to David, where she must share her home and David's love with six other women.[13]

We imagine resentment continued to mount in Michal's heart, and the chasm between her and David widened when he allowed the Gibeonites to kill seven of her remaining brothers and nephews (2 Samuel 21:5–6). Surely wave upon wave of grief consumed Michal at this point. Her life had not turned out as she planned. At every turn she seemed to experience painful, heartbreaking loss. And every grief she experienced seemed connected to David. Every blow to her heart involved him.

It all came to a head the day David danced into town. He had gone to Obed-Edom's house to retrieve the ark of the covenant. He was thrilled that it was being returned to its rightful place, and he danced with unbridled enthusiasm, worshipping God with abandoned exuberance. Passion oozed from his very pores as he celebrated with all his strength.

Second Samuel 6:14–23 tells it like this:

And David danced before the LORD with all his might, wearing a priestly garment. So David and all the people of Israel brought up the Ark of the LORD with shouts of joy and the blowing of rams' horns.

But as the Ark of the LORD entered the City of David, Michal, the daughter of Saul, looked down from her window. When she saw King David leaping and dancing before the Lord, she was filled with contempt for him.

They brought the Ark of the LORD and set it in its place inside the special tent David had prepared for it. And David sacrificed burnt offerings and peace offerings to the LORD. When he had finished his sacrifices, David blessed the people in the name of the LORD of Heaven's Armies. Then he gave to every Israelite man and woman in the crowd a loaf of bread, a cake of dates, and a cake of raisins. Then all the people returned to their homes.

When David returned home to bless his own family, Michal, the daughter of Saul, came out to meet him. She said in disgust, "How distinguished the king of Israel looked today, shamelessly exposing himself to the servant girls like any vulgar person might do!"

David retorted to Michal, "I was dancing before the LORD, who chose me above your father and all his family! He appointed me as the leader of Israel, the people of the LORD, so I celebrate before the LORD. Yes, and I am willing to look even more foolish than this, even to be humiliated in my own eyes! But those servant girls you mentioned will indeed think I am distinguished!"

So Michal, the daughter of Saul, remained childless throughout her entire life.

As Michal sat perched in the window watching David dance in the streets, her heart burned with contempt and disdain. She despised him and his behavior. We're pretty sure this had nothing to do with the day's events and everything to do with their history together. We think she despised him long before he twirled into Jerusalem that day.

It's not clear where we got the popular idea that David was naked or even in his underwear. This passage clearly states that he was wearing a "priestly garment." We can assure you, there is nothing indecent about a priestly garment. It's also no secret that in Jewish culture there's a lot of dancing. (Have you seen *Fiddler on the Roof?*) There was nothing wrong with anything David did. But in Michal's *opinion* (my-my-my), David was neither appropriately dressed, nor was he behaving like a proper sovereign should. She felt empowered to hold such critical opinions because she despised him.

We know it's been said that Michal's contempt was rooted in self-importance and arrogance. We've read the commentaries that say she had hell in her heart and exhibited contemptuous pride. We are not theologians, but in our estimation, Michal had such a negative opinion of David's behavior and attire because she held unforgiveness toward him. Her problem was not with priestly garments or uninhibited worship of God. While there may have been pride, arrogance, and self-importance in her heart, her real problem

> ⓖ
>
> *Her real problem was years of repressed pain, hurt, and grief that had been piled upon her wounded heart.*

was years of repressed pain, hurt, and grief that had been piled upon her wounded heart. This bitterness and anger bubbled to the surface, spilling over in the form of criticism as she watched David dance with joy. Her soul, imprisoned by unforgiveness, rebelled at such a bold display of freedom. In her anger, she minced no words as she expressed extreme displeasure and disapproval, passionately berating him.

Her story doesn't end well. David closed the door on their relationship, and they remained estranged for the rest of her life. Going forward, she was identified as the "daughter of Saul," instead of the "wife of David" (2 Samuel 6:23). She ended life barren and childless, alone and lonely.

The lesson we learn from the history of Michal, daughter of Saul, is this: unforgiveness not only breeds anger and resentment, it fosters criticism. We certainly understand why Michal would be so wounded. There's no doubt that she would have been terribly hurt and angry. We can see how she would have come to resent David, possibly even giving her father's share of the blame to David. We understand. But instead of processing through her pain with God and allowing Him to heal these deep wounds by embracing forgiveness, she hung on to every offense, letting them grow and fester in her heart until her tongue easily spoke the language of anger and resentment—criticism.

While there is much to learn from Michal, we think the biggest lesson of all is the connection between unforgiveness and criticism. Anger and resentment are the main tentacles on the root of all criticism. And unforgiveness is like fertilizer for the ravenous roots of anger, leading us along the treacherous path of criticism. Sadly, the results are barrenness. Criticism creates a place void of intimacy where nothing can grow.

Michal's story is heartbreaking. However, it's not wasted if we learn from it. Before you move on to the final history lesson, take some time to meander through her story and see what lessons you can learn.

11

THE RAGING CRITICS

We like to imagine that it was a warm summer day when Jesus walked into Nazareth. He'd been on the western shores of Galilee announcing the arrival of the Kingdom of God, and now He was headed home to ensure His people knew about its coming as well. We assume the townsfolk would have been happy to see Him again. They had watched Him grow up as a child, and they knew Him to be a gentle, kind, and good-natured boy. Surely they had missed His smiling face and pleasant demeanor around town. Don't you think He had many friends and the people of Nazareth loved Him?

During that time, it was common for laypeople to participate in synagogue services, especially reading from the scrolls containing sacred text. Visiting rabbis could also be invited to provide a message. They likely eagerly invited Jesus, the native son they enjoyed so much, to speak at the weekly service. Anxious to hear what He had to say, they sat attentive, taking in every word. As wisdom and revelation began to flow from Him, they were astonished. His miraculous powers overwhelmed them. They had not expected to hear such insight delivered with such authority from one of their own.

But as He continued to teach, their astonishment turned into contempt and mockery. They couldn't believe the little boy they had watched grow up could be so . . . so . . . profound. So authoritative. So powerful.

This event is chronicled in Matthew 13:53–58, Mark 6:1–6, and Luke 4:14–30. We're going to feature Matthew's account because, as noted before, Bill has great partiality for the book of Matthew.

When Jesus had finished telling these stories and illustrations, he left that part of the country. He returned to Nazareth, his hometown. When he taught there in the synagogue, everyone was amazed and said, "Where does he get this wisdom and the power to do miracles?" Then they scoffed, "He's just the carpenter's son, and we know Mary, his mother, and his brothers—James, Joseph, Simon, and Judas. All his sisters live right here among us. Where did he learn all these things?" And they were deeply offended and refused to believe in him.

Then Jesus told them, "A prophet is honored everywhere except in his own hometown and among his own family." And so he did only a few miracles there because of their unbelief.

It's hard for us to believe they would view Jesus in this way. They were experiencing what so many of us long for: to hear Jesus teach in person. They were listening to Him deliver deep truths with their own ears. They were in the same room with Him. They could feel the impact of His words and sense His authority. They could see the love and compassion pouring from His heart. They could hear the tones of mercy in His voice. How could they have seen all this and still miss the fact that the long-awaited Messiah was in their very midst? How could they have been so harsh toward Him? How could they have turned on Him so quickly?

> As they sat there listening to the wonders of the Kingdom being announced with an open invitation to join, their inner critics began to scream.

Easy. They had critical spirits. As they sat there listening to the wonders of the Kingdom being announced with an open invitation to join, their inner critics began to scream. *What is this? We know Him. He's just a carpenter's son. He's nothing special. We know His family; they are average people, just like us. How could He possibly be different? We were taught the same things He was taught. We studied in this very synagogue with Him. Where would He have learned that? How could He know anything about these things? Why would He presume to know that? Who does He think He is? What right does He have to say such things? We will not listen to this. We will not believe anything He is saying. We will not tolerate His presence.* Can you hear their harsh tone, bathed in ridicule with a touch of sarcasm?

As they sat there, hurling criticisms at Him, offense began to grow in their hearts. They took umbrage at His wisdom. They resented His authority. They felt insulted by the depths of revelation that flowed from Him because they had presumed He was ordinary, just like them. They resented the fact that He was different. More. Other. It offended them.

There is so much to see and learn in this passage. But we've narrowed it down to three key points that apply to the context of this book.

Their criticism kept them from seeing and recognizing truth. Because criticism was their default setting, they immediately ridiculed Jesus. This instantly put them on the defensive, causing them to be cynical. Criticism put blinders on their eyes and prevented them from recognizing that He, indeed, was different from them—He was the Son of God, the long-awaited Messiah.

Criticism was the hothouse that allowed offense to grow. A critical heart offers the perfect growing conditions for resentment, indignation, and anger to thrive. Once they began to criticize Jesus, offense was the natural outcome. A critical spirit is easily offended by anything. Even the most innocent action rubs a critical spirit the wrong way, causing us to be upset, insulted, and assume the worst.

The critical path led directly to a roadblock. Their criticism led to offense, which took them right into unbelief. Their unbelief was the barrier that prevented them from experiencing the miracles Jesus longed to give them. It was obviously hard for them to trust Jesus when their hearts were full of criticism of Him.

Our biggest takeaway from this historical event is this: criticism causes offense and creates mistrust, which prevents our hearts from being open to possibilities. Whether we are talking about our relationship with Jesus, with our spouses, or any other relationships in our lives, criticism will throw up a roadblock that prevents us from experiencing all the relationship has to offer. It keeps us from receiving anything from the relationship. It limits the beautiful ways the relationship can grow and flourish. It stunts potential and cripples opportunity for intimacy and authenticity.

It is said that history repeats itself because no one was listening the first time. May we all strive to become avid learners, not only of history, but of the ever-present events unfolding around us, by looking at everything through the eyes of Jesus. Only then will we advance to new heights and greater rewards.

Part**Three**

The Challenge

THE COMPLAINING CHALLENGE

PREPARING FOR THE CHALLENGE

The first step of any challenge is to get your gear in order. To help, we've compiled a list of things you'll need to have and do in order to squeeze every ounce of adventure from this experience.

First and foremost, pray. If you attempt this Challenge apart from prayer, it will crush you. As negativity surfaces from hidden places in your life, you'll be overwhelmed and discouraged. You'll be shocked with awareness. It's important to talk to Father God about everything as you journey through. Talk about your thoughts, attitudes, and words. Talk to Him about how you feel and what stings, offends, or makes you angry. Talk with Him about what breaks your heart as realization dawns on you. Ask Jesus to journey with you, exposing lies, revealing truth, and healing wounds as you go. Ask Holy Spirit for insight, clarity, and revelation. Invite Him into every aspect of this adventure. It will make the difference between success and failure.

Next, understand this will be a process. You did not wire your brain for negativity and build a stronghold over night. It will take more than one day—more than seven days!—to demolish the stronghold, rewire your brain, and establish a fortress of truth. If you complain, criticize, or argue at any point during this Challenge, you are not a failure. Don't give up! Process with Jesus. Regroup. Learn. And, then, move on. The only way you can fail is if you quit.

Finally, travel slowly. Don't read all seven days at once. Take it day by day, and do the work assigned each day. Answer all the questions. Be authentic. This is between you and Jesus, and He already knows all the sordid details anyway. So be real. You'll never get anywhere if you aren't truthful about where you are. Write your answers in the spaces provided or record them in a journal—don't just answer them in your head. Record everything God is showing you. Highlight, underline, and make notes in the margins. At the end of your day, ask yourself the Reflection Questions. These are designed to help you think through your day and evaluate your progress. Dig deep. Be honest and you'll be amazed!

We encourage you to take this Challenge in the way that works best for you. Every person's journey is different, so don't think you've failed if you don't complete it in seven days. This is intense, and you may want more than one day to focus on each assignment. That's fine! In fact, the slower you go, the deeper you dig, the more lasting the change will be. Get the most out of the experience.

YOUR TOOLS FOR THE JOURNEY

A Bible

You will need a Bible to look up the Scriptures in each day's work. Even if they're familiar to you, approach them from the perspective of what you don't know about them. We assure you, there is way more you don't know about them than you do.

Scripture was written by Holy Spirit. Second Timothy 3:16 (TPT) says, "Every Scripture has been written by the Holy Spirit, the breath of God. It will empower you by its instruction and correction, giving you the strength to take the right direction and lead you deeper into the path of godliness." When we read the Bible, we are humans attempting to understand divine things, which is virtually impossible without the help of the Divine One. We ask Holy Spirit for revelation and understanding. We need Him to interpret what we're reading. As the Author, He knows precisely what the meaning and intent of every word is. Look to Him to deepen, expand, and explain the truth to you.

Come to Scripture expecting to see something new. Expect to find treasure. Invest time to meditate. Soak your heart in the words, and turn them over in your mind. Ruminate! Look at them from all angles. Read them in other translations. This can give you great insight and bring tremendous clarity. Ask yourself these questions when meditating on verses:

- What do these verses mean to me personally?

- How do they apply to my life?

- How do my current actions line up with that truth?

- What would it look like to live this truth out?

- How would my life change if I applied this truth?

Note: throughout the guide, we occasionally specify a particular translation or paraphrase by noting it in parentheses immediately following the verse. We believe that specific translation will give you unique insight and clarity to our point. If you don't own that translation, no worries! You can easily find them on the YouVersion Bible app or the website Bible Gateway (www.biblegateway.com). Both of these tools are great resources we each use frequently, and we are sure you will find them helpful.

TRANSLATION KEY

NLT – New Living Translation
AMP – Amplified Version
TPT – The Passion Translation

A Journal

You also need a journal. Whether it's a notebook, legal pad, or a fine leather journal, you need something to write in. In case you haven't noticed, we're big on writing stuff down. Writing helps us to remember. The better and more detailed our notes are, the more likely we are to remember. Plus, you can go back and read the insight and revelation again and again as you work through future issues.

Ask God to speak to you and write in detail what He is saying to you through each day's lesson. What is He revealing through the verses you meditate on? What do you see as you ask yourself questions about those verses that we mentioned in the paragraph above? What are the insights Holy Spirit is giving you? Be as thorough as you can possibly be. No matter how profound the revelation, you will eventually forget it. Writing it down will ensure you have it for future reference and reflection.

A Partner

Finally, get a partner. Accountability and transparency are key components to success. Find someone to journey with, someone you can be "real" with, someone who will encourage you, support you, and cheer you on. Don't get a "yes man." That won't do you any good. Instead, find someone who is brutally—but lovingly—honest with you. (And someone you can be brutally—but lovingly—honest with too.) You will need this type of support for the long haul. We suggest that you meet nightly with your accountability partner during the Challenge. Grab coffee, chat by phone, FaceTime, text, or do a Google hangout. If your accountability partner is not your spouse, we highly recommend they be the same gender you are. It's just wiser and safer that way!

One last suggestion before you start the Challenge: fast. Biblical fasting is abstaining from food and replacing that meal with prayer for the purpose of burrowing deeper into the heart of God so you experience clarity. This is not a requirement for the Challenge, but it is a suggestion we make. It is a powerful tool to help you see God clearly and hear the voice of Jesus plainly.

HOW TO USE THIS GUIDE

We designed each day with four sections: Study, Activation, Reflection, and Accountability. You can do the Study and Activation together or separately. However, we recommend you do the Reflection separately from the other sections, preferably in the evening. Pick the time that's best for you, when you are not rushed, to ensure you fully absorb what you're reading and can hear and see what Holy Spirit is showing you. Preparation is key. If you just try to work it in to your day, it probably won't happen.

If you'll prepare and step into the Challenge with a desire to experience life-long change, it *will* change your life. And your marriage, family dynamics, kids, job, relationships: everything. But you actually have to do the work with a fully engaged heart for change to occur. Going through the motions will get you nothing but disappointment.

So, this is it. We commit to abstaining from complaining for the next seven days. We are choosing not to complain, grumble, fuss, gripe, growl, criticize, find fault, cast blame, argue, or express discontent, disgust, annoyance, or frustration about anything or anyone. This includes, but is not limited to, statements such as:

- I don't like . . .

- I wish . . .

- I can't wait until . . .

- I'm so tired of . . .

- They make me . . .

- If only . . .

- Why do they . . .

- and anything else that sounds like this!

No subject is exempt. There are no exceptions. Not your spouse. Your ex. Kids. Family. Job. Boss. Co-workers. Income. Health. Bills. Neighbors. Church. Hair. Body. Clothes. Food. House. Laundry. Dishes. Weather. Government. Media. Or, any decisions made by anyone, anywhere at any time. Just to name a few things.

We will not *think* it. We will not *say* it. If we do either, we choose to immediately stop, confess, and repent.

Process through your feelings with Jesus and ask Him to change your heart. Ask Him to let you see people through His eyes. Ask Him to show you the situation through His perspective. Ask Him to show you His fingerprints in your circumstances: The good. The promise. The blessing. Ask Him to shift your perception. Ask Him to reveal the root of the complaint or criticism.

Then, ask Him to show you something to be grateful for—even if it's just one thing. As you choose to reject every complaint and criticism, replace them with gratitude and thankfulness.

You may be thinking, *this is impossible.* But remember what we said in chapter five: with God, all things are possible! God would never instruct us to do something like this alone. He is fully prepared and equipped to help you remove complaining, criticizing, and arguing from your thinking and language. Not only is He prepared, but He wants to help. Philippians 2:13 says, "For God is working in you, giving you the desire and the power to do what pleases him." He is setting us up for success!

Are you ready?

The pre-challenge workout is next!

PRE-CHALLENGE WORKOUTS

Before you start a workout, you stretch to prepare yourself for endurance. We have two great exercises that are an excellent way to stretch your soul in order to prepare yourself for the long haul of this Challenge.

Stretching Exercise #1: Ask, "Do I . . ."

They say that admitting you have a problem is the first step to fixing the problem. With that in mind, before you start, spend time talking with Holy Spirit, asking Him if you have a mouth problem. You don't know what you don't know, and only He can clearly show you if you do. So, ask.

Ask if you are speaking the enemy's language. Ask Him to show you if you are carelessly tossing out complaining, critical, or argumentative words that you are unaware of. Ask Him to show you the words that fill your life. Ask if life or death is the fruit of your tongue.

We find it's helpful to have God's perspective on a subject before we try to institute any change. Stretch deep, no matter how painful it is. Don't rush through. Don't assume you know the answer. What He reveals to you here will be instrumental to your success in the challenge.

Write everything He shows you here.

_____

_____

_____

_____

_____

_____

_____

_____

_____

_____

_____

_____

_____

_____

_____

_____

_____

_____

_____

_____

Stretching Exercise #2: Ask, "What if . . ."

To ask "what if" is to wonder what could happen should a particular action or habit in your life change. In this exercise, you will consider how things could be different should change be implemented. You'll speculate about what could happen in the future and imagine possibilities.

We believe "what if" is one of the most powerful questions you could ever ask yourself. "What if" questions compel us to imagine, explore, and create. "What if" questions require us to search, investigate, and discover more about ourselves and about God. By asking "what if" questions, we challenge the lies we believe and open the door for truth to invade that space. "What if" questions highlight opportunities for more and produce a yearning for better, and greater. They make room for hope, filling us with anticipation and expectancy. "What if" questions are full of possibilities.

They motivate us, churning desire, making us hungry for change, and moving us to action. They invite us to shed the status quo. They open our eyes to potential and awaken dreams within us.

Because "what if" questions are so powerful, they are the optimal tool to use when implementing change. Since the focus of this book is to help you step into change by eliminating complaining and criticism, asking "what if" questions related to this Challenge is a helpful exercise.

First, make a list of your "what if" questions in the space below. Think specifically about eliminating complaints from your life, and think about the "what if"s that could happen if you do. We've listed some examples of "what if" questions you may want to ask. However, partner with Holy Spirit, asking him to bring the right questions to mind for you.

- What if I stopped internally criticizing my spouse?

- What if I stopped focusing on my spouse's annoying habits and started intentionally focusing on their good qualities?

- What if I stopped complaining about my children?

- What if I started appreciating the season my children are in?

- What if I stopped complaining about my job? My boss? My co-workers?

- What if I started appreciating the benefits of my job?

- What if I stopped criticizing my body? My personality?

- What if I stopped comparing myself to others?

- What if I began to appreciate and find value in my uniqueness?

- What if I stopped focusing on what I can't do and focused on what I can do?

- What if I stopped complaining about the weather?

- What if I expressed thankfulness for my home in every season?

- What if I intentionally looked for—searched for—good things in people and situations?

Next, think through the possibilities your "what if" questions raise. Picture yourself living in that situation. How would that change your emotions? Your marriage? Your relationships? Your career? Allow yourself to mentally go with Holy Spirit in every direction He leads you, as far into the future as possible. Then, consider doing nothing and ignoring the "what if." Weed through the scenarios you imagine with Him until you land on your ideal answer. Then write it down. Ask Holy Spirit His thoughts on the outcome and write that down as well.

Finally, you're going to make a declaration. A declaration is a proclamation, a decree, or an announcement of how things will be in the future. Think of the Declaration of Independence. This document was an announcement made by the thirteen colonies to England, stating that a change was being made. From that point forward, things would be different. They proclaimed to the world that from that day onward, they would function in the manner outlined in the document and they would not deviate from it. It was an emphatic declaration that was birthed from a group of men who asked, "what if?"

Declarations help anchor your resolve. When they are done in partnership with Holy Spirit, they are powerful, life-changing proclamations that tear down strongholds and establish new fortresses of truth in your brain. Declarations are powerful tools for re-wiring your brain. If you want to change, ask "what if" and then confidently declare the answer.

For example, if you were to ask, "What if I were to focus only on my spouse's good qualities?" you'd think through ways your relationship might change. Holy Spirit might lead you to Scriptures that correlate with your desire to think differently about your spouse. This is important because the power-packed punch of a declaration comes from the truth woven into it.

From there, you might form a declaration statement that looks like this:

I declare that I love ___, and love always acts in patience, is never irritable, and holds no record of wrongs. Therefore, I choose to forgive ___ like Jesus has forgiven me, and I will be tenderhearted toward him/her. I choose to reject rude thoughts and comments, replacing them with kind thoughts and gentle words, as I abandon every display of selfishness and express a greater concern for what matters to him/her. As I live in love, I declare that we will put to rest any division that attempts to tear us apart, and we will be restored as one united body living in perfect harmony with a common perspective and shared values.[14]

Finally, we encourage you to say your declaration out loud. There is power in verbally declaring truth. It has a greater impact on you emotionally, physically, and spiritually. So, say your declarations out loud. Say them in the shower. Say them in the car. Say them as you mow the lawn, rake the leaves, and fold the clothes. Say them when your emotions are cheering you on and when they aren't. Say it to remind yourself that, from this moment forward, you will function in a manner that lines up with truth. Say it emphatically, declaring you will not deviate from it. Say it out loud and say it like you mean it.

This exercise may take you awhile. You may need to do this over the course of several days. You may need more space than we've allotted for it below. That's okay. Use your journal or notebook. Take your time. Deep change cannot be rushed.

What if _____

_____

_____

_____

The results would be _____

_____

_____

_____

My declaration _____

_____

_____

_____

What if _____

_____

_____

_____

The results would be _____

_____

_____

_____

My declaration _____

_____

_____

_____

_____

What if _____

_____

_____

_____

The results would be _____

_____

_____

_____

My declaration _____

_____

_____

_____

What if _____

_____

_____

_____

The results would be _____

_____

_____

_____

My declaration _____

_____

_____

_____

What if _____

_____

_____

_____

The results would be _____

_____

_____

_____

My declaration _____

_____

_____

_____

What if _____

_____

_____

_____

The results would be _____

_____

_____

_____

My declaration _____

_____

_____

_____

_____

THE COMPLAINING CURE

What if _____

_____

_____

_____

The results would be _____

_____

_____

_____

My declaration _____

_____

_____

_____

What if _____

_____

_____

_____

The results would be _____

_____

_____

_____

My declaration _____

_____

_____

_____

DAY 1

TODAY'S CHALLENGE :

Inspect thoughts to discover how unforgiveness influences them.

STUDY

So, let's talk about our thoughts, because that's where words start. Our words are shaped by our attitudes. An *attitude* (or *mind-set*) is "a habitual, typical, and normal thought process that determines how you will interpret (understand and receive) the information and situations you encounter, and it dictates how you will respond to that information and those situations." These patterns of thinking establish our perspective and create the lens through which we see life.

(That paragraph is full of important information. In fact, we recommend you read it several times before moving on.)

Our normal thought process and perspective forms the words we say. We never *accidently* say anything. Everything we say originates from our attitude. Every word was formed by our thoughts. Jesus said it this way in Luke 6:45, "What you say flows from what is in your heart." In the original Greek, the word "heart" is *kardia*, and it means "the heart, mind, and inner life." Every single word you speak was thought through and established in your mind before it was broadcast from your mouth. They are premeditated. Remember what we said in chapter 2 about neural pathways? Your brain can do things more quickly than you realize!

If we want to be free from complaining and criticizing, we must first address our thoughts. We've got to deal with what's going on in our hearts before we can ever tackle what's coming out of our mouths. When our hearts are full of envy, resentment, bitterness, and offense, our language easily converts to complaining, and criticism.

Dealing with negative attitudes is critical when uprooting complaining from your life. The foundation of negativity is unforgiveness. Unforgiveness creates prison bars that trap us with toxic thinking and poisonous words. Sadly, the contaminated words often bleed out into other aspects of our thinking and conversations too.

There's only one key that can free us from the prison of unforgiveness, and that is forgiveness. There is no other way to dismantle the bars that entrap us.

We think Peter must have struggled with unforgiveness, because he asked Jesus how to handle a repeat offender. That's a tough one, don't you think? Here's the account in Matthew 18:21–35:

Then Peter came to him and asked, "Lord, how often should I forgive someone who sins against me? Seven times?"

"No, not seven times," Jesus replied, "but seventy times seven!"

Therefore, the Kingdom of Heaven can be compared to a king who decided to bring his accounts up to date with servants who had borrowed money from him. In the process, one of his debtors was brought in who owed him millions of dollars. He couldn't pay, so his master ordered that he be sold—along with his wife, his children, and everything he owned—to pay the debt.

"But the man fell down before his master and begged him, 'Please, be patient with me, and I will pay it all.' Then his master was filled with pity for him, and he released him and forgave his debt.

"But when the man left the king, he went to a fellow servant who owed him a few thousand dollars. He grabbed him by the throat and demanded instant payment.

"His fellow servant fell down before him and begged for a little more time. 'Be patient with me, and I will pay it,' he pleaded. But his creditor wouldn't wait. He had the man arrested and put in prison until the debt could be paid in full.

"When some of the other servants saw this, they were very upset. They went to the king and told him everything that had happened. Then the king called in the man he had forgiven and said, 'You evil servant! I forgave you that tremendous debt because you pleaded with me. Shouldn't you have mercy on your fellow servant, just as I had mercy on you?' Then the angry king sent the man to prison to be tortured until he had paid his entire debt.

"That's what my heavenly Father will do to you if you refuse to forgive your brothers and sisters from your heart."

Forgiveness frees you from the prison unforgiveness creates with all its entanglements, like damaging attitudes and poisonous words. We do not pretend this is easy. Many of us carry deep wounds that harbor unforgiveness, both consciously and subconsciously. Many of us, like Peter, have repeat offenders in our lives. But if we are ever going to be free from complaining, then we have to process those wounds with Jesus and let Him clean them out and heal us. As He does this, resentment, bitterness, anger, and offense fall away and no longer have influence over our thoughts and words. Instead, Holy Spirit influences our thinking and we find we no longer want to complain or criticize.

Change is an inside job. The key to freedom is not to focus on changing your behavior, but on changing your heart. When your heart is free and in alignment with His, change becomes evident on the outside.

So today, your challenge is to inspect your heart for unforgiveness. Ask Holy Spirit to reveal to you any area where unforgiveness is hiding and how it has influenced your thoughts, attitudes, and words.

Begin your conversation with Him by reading Psalm 139:23–24 out loud: "Search me, O God, and know my heart; test me and know my anxious thoughts. Point out anything in me that offends you, and lead me along the path of everlasting life."

Then listen. He will bring things to your mind because He wants you to be free more than you want to be free. He will not overwhelm you or give you more than you can handle. He may take several days or weeks to unearth pockets of unforgiveness as He speaks to you during your quiet time. Memories may begin to surface or Holy Spirit may reveal something to you in a dream. However long it takes and however He chooses to reveal it to you, be willing to partner with Him to freedom.

As you allowed God to search your heart, what did He reveal?

_____

_____

_____

Did this revelation surprise you? Why do you think it did or did not?

_____

_____

_____

ACTIVATION

This section of our journey is crucial. Too often we read or hear God's Truth, agree with it, and understand that we need to apply it in our lives—but stop there. We never take the next step to activate that truth in our lives. This section is intended to help you activate what you're reading and hearing from God on this journey.

Each day you will look up the Scriptures listed and spend time meditating on them, looking at them from every angle and thinking through how you can apply them to your life. Biblical meditation involves filling your mind with the verse and letting it expand and unfold until your mind is overflowing. It's important to journal what you see and hear, as well as what steps you can take to implement these verses in your life.

Following the verses, we will ask questions designed to help you apply what you read in the Study section. Take your time, because the more you invest here, the easier it will be to walk it out.

READ

Colossians 3:13, Ephesians 4:31–32, Luke 6:43–45, Proverbs 27:19, and Proverbs 4:23. Journal in detail what Holy Spirit is showing you for each verse.

ANSWER

Before you quickly jot down an answer to these questions, think about what they will mean for you and all they could entail.

1. What do you hope to accomplish during this Challenge? What do you want to see changed in you?

   _____

   _____

   _____

   _____

2. Are you willing to let Holy Spirit expose complaints and criticism in your life? Even aspects that may be hidden in plain sight? Those things you've always done? Write your thought process out.

   _____

   _____

   _____

   _____

3. What thoughts do you have that are connected to jealousy, envy, resentment, dissatisfaction, bitterness, anger, and offense?

   _____

   _____

   _____

4. Which of these seem to be the biggest influence on you and why?

_____

_____

_____

5. Ask Holy Spirit if you have been imprisoned by unforgiveness. Ask Him to show you the prison bars. What do you hear and see?

_____

_____

_____

6. Are you willing to let Holy Spirit expose unforgiveness in your life? Even toward people or situations where it seems justified?

_____

_____

_____

PRAY

If you find you don't know where to start as you begin to forgive people who hurt you, we have a prayer to help you along the way. If you really struggle with unforgiveness, we recommend you find additional resources on forgiveness to help you process through to the freedom that is yours in Jesus. It's too important not to deal with it thoroughly!

A Prayer for Forgiving Others

Father, I choose to forgive [name].
I forgive them for [what they did to hurt you].
I believe they owe me the debt of [name what you feel you lost or were owed],
and before You, I release them from this debt.

I completely release them to You.
You are the only One who has the right and authority
to hold them accountable for what they did.
You are the only One who can judge them for their words and actions.
I give the case file for them and this situation to You
so that You can deal with them as You see fit.

Jesus, heal my wounded heart and my bruised emotions so I can love them.
Dismantle the prison I have built for myself
because of unforgiveness and bitterness toward them.
Tear down this prison so that I am totally free
and will no longer shut people out of my life due to unforgiveness.
Please bring peace to my heart so when I remember what they did,
or when I am in their presence, I will be filled with Your peace and Your love.
Amen

Now go out there and make it a great day! And remember, no complaining about anything!

REFLECTION

It's now the end of your first full day of the Challenge, so let's do some observation. Reflection gives Holy Spirit room to encourage us and course correct us as needed! Remember, it's just Day 1. So, you may not have anything remarkable to report. That's okay! The purpose is to practice introspection in conjunction with Holy Spirit.

As you inspected your thoughts, what type of thoughts did you find?

_____

_____

_____

_____

What type of patterns did you notice regarding complaining, criticism, and arguing?

_____

_____

_____

_____

How often did you have complaining or critical thoughts but did not express them?

_____

_____

_____

_____

Did you say something without realizing you were expressing your thoughts out loud?

_____

_____

_____

_____

Prayer

Father God,

I confess to You that I have complaining, critical, and argumentative thoughts that stem from unforgiveness. These attitudes have been in my thoughts for so long that I can't recognize them—they've become normal. Forgive me for hanging on to offense and allowing it to take root in my heart. I give You permission to reveal all thoughts that are entangled with jealousy, envy, resentment, dissatisfaction, bitterness, anger, offense, and any other negative emotion connected to unforgiveness. Expose areas of barrenness that are the results of complaining and criticism. I ask You to show me how they are connected to unforgiveness so that I can choose to forgive. Give me a heart that desires to forgive and the strength to do it.

Amen

As you close out the day, know that you are not alone. Jesus is fighting for you, Holy Spirit is empowering you, and Father God is with you. Plus, we're on your side, cheering you on and praying for you. So, you got this! Victory is yours!

ACCOUNTABILITY

Don't forget to connect with your accountability partner! Discuss the challenges of rewiring your brain. Share your doubts and expectations. Talk about your hesitancy and excitement. Share your declaration statement with them. You'll be surprised at how motivating, honest, and transparent conversations really are!

"A friendly discussion is as stimulating as the sparks that fly when iron strikes iron." (Proverbs 27:17 TLB)

DAY 2

TODAY'S CHALLENGE :

Take thoughts captive through surrender and submission.

STUDY

Congrats! You survived the first day! And you're back for round two, which means you're headed down the road to success. We're proud of you and admire your willingness to tackle this mountain in your life!

Yesterday we looked at how important our thoughts are and how our thoughts form our words. So, this Challenge is about more than just keeping our mouths closed. It's really about changing the way we think.

Changing the way you think primarily comes through surrender and submission. Romans 12:1–2 explains it like this:

And so, dear brothers and sisters, I plead with you to give your bodies to God because of all he has done for you. Let them be a living and holy sacrifice—the kind he will find acceptable. This is truly the way to worship him. Don't copy the behavior and customs of this world, but let God transform you into a new person by changing the way you think.

As we surrender our bodies (which includes our minds, tongues, and mouths) we are sacrificing our opinions, perceptions, and desires to Jesus. He meets us at the altar of sacrifice and exchanges what we surrendered with His perspective. As we live in total surrender and complete submission to His Lordship, allowing Him to weave His character into our soul, we'll no longer *want* to think like the world around us. Instead of letting society form our opinions, adopting the culture's language and conforming to society's attitude, we'll begin to adopt His heart and perspective.

As our thinking changes, we experience transformation: radical, revolutionary, and deep-seated transformation. Through surrender, we begin to see the world through His eyes, hear everything through His ears, and feel it all through His heart. In that revelation, our thoughts evolve, as the mind of Christ is made manifest in our lives. Thinking with the mind of Christ will naturally transform our thoughts, which in turn, transforms our words. Change comes from inside a heart that has been completely surrendered and lives in submission to Him.

Soaking our hearts in truth also fosters transformation. Never underestimate the value of reading the Bible. We read in 2 Timothy 3:16–17 (TPT) that:

Every Scripture has been written by the Holy Spirit, the breath of God. It will empower you by its instruction and correction, giving you the strength to take the right direction and lead you deeper into the path of godliness. Then you will be God's servant, fully mature and perfectly prepared to fulfill any assignment God gives you.

And Hebrews 4:12 (TPT) says:

We have the living Word of God, which is full of energy, and it pierces more sharply than a two-edged sword. It will even penetrate to the very core of our being where soul and spirit, bone and marrow meet! It interprets and reveals the true thoughts and secret motives of our hearts.

As we read the Word of God, it reveals where our thinking is out of line with Jesus and tells us what He thinks. The Bible makes us more aware of who He is, revealing to us who we are supposed to be. It is critical in the transformation process.

Another way to promote transformation is to aggressively assault the stronghold of complaining and critical thinking. Change comes as we disassemble the well-fortified fortress in our minds that is dominated by the enemy and allows him tremendous influence in that area of our lives.

In 2 Corinthians 10:5 (AMP) we read, "We are destroying sophisticated arguments and every exalted and proud thing that sets itself up against the [true] knowledge of God, and we are taking every thought and purpose captive to the obedience of Christ." We can't allow ourselves to go on autopilot any more. We must be aware of the thoughts that are filling our minds.

This means we cannot let our thoughts run rampant. We can't let them roam, idly daydream, or create fantasies. We usually do this because we are unhappy or dissatisfied with something in our lives, and that brings us to criticism. We must be intentional with our thinking. We've got to listen to what's going on in our heads. This means we must take every thought captive.

To do this, we'll need to inspect and interrogate every thought. And we mean every thought. Asking questions is a great way to examine your thoughts. Imagine an internal dialogue with each thought like this:

- Where did you come from?

- Do you sound like Jesus? Are you loving or kind?

- Or, do you sound like the enemy? Judgmental? Accusing? Envious? Harsh?

- How do you make me feel? Encouraged? Peaceful? Hopeful? Loving?

- Or, do you make me feel irritated? Frustrated? Resentful? Angry?

- Do you line up with the Bible?

If you find thoughts that are negative in any way, give them to Jesus. Surrender them to Him and ask Him to take them and give you His perspective in exchange.

Don't ignore or repress any thought. Address them head on, deal with them, and eliminate them. Don't assume anything is "approved building material" for the fortress of truth you are establishing in your brain just because it's normal for you or anybody else. Inspect every thought with a microscope. If it doesn't meet the specs of truth, stop it and take it captive. Don't let it become a brick in the wall of the complaining stronghold.

As we take every thought captive, we'll be tearing down that stronghold brick by brick.

Today, the challenge is surrendering to Jesus. Not just thoughts and words, but everything. Take every aspect of your being and relinquish control. Be intentional to take your hands off the wheel, and give Him permission to take complete control. Then, choose to submit. In an act of trust, forfeit your rights—your thoughts, attitudes, and words—and embrace His Lordship in your life.

What is the correlation between change, and surrender and submission?

_____

_____

_____

_____

_____

How do you normally handle negative situations and hurtful encounters?

_____

_____

_____

_____

_____

ACTIVATION

Sir Isaac Newton was a mathematician, physicist, astronomer, and theologian who was a key figure in the scientific revolution of the seventeenth century. His First Law of Motion describes *inertia*. According to this law, a body at rest tends to stay at rest, and a body in motion tends to stay in motion. It's important to set truth into motion in our lives. Look up these verses and think through how you can implement them into your life so that you stay in forward motion!

READ

Romans 12:1–2, Ephesians 4:21–24, 2 Corinthians 10:3–6 and 1 Peter 1:13–16. Journal everything you discover as Holy Spirit shines light on these verses.

ANSWER

1. How do you feel about surrender and submission?

   _____

   _____

   _____

   _____

2. How can you better partner with Holy Spirit to renew your thoughts?

   _____

   _____

   _____

   _____

3. In what areas of your thought life does the enemy strategically work to fortify the stronghold he operates in your thinking?

_____

_____

_____

_____

4. How did it feel to take complaining, critical, and argumentative thoughts captive? To take control of your thoughts?

_____

_____

_____

_____

Start your day by boldly proclaiming your declaration statement. Now go out there and crush complaining!

REFLECTION

It's the second night, and you may not feel like you have anything positive to report yet, but that's not true! Even Holy Spirit's conviction of complaining and critical thoughts is a success. It means you are one step closer to freedom!

How often did you go on autopilot, daydream, or have unchecked thoughts running loose in your head?

_____

_____

_____

Did you try to ignore or repress any thoughts?

_____

_____

_____

How aware were you of your thoughts today?

_____

_____

_____

What changes did you notice when you took thoughts captive?

_____

_____

_____

_____

Prayer

Father God,

I confess to you that I have established patterns of complaining and critical thinking. I repent for letting them roam freely in my mind and allowing them to influence and control my words.

I no longer want them to have free reign, so I choose to surrender them and submit to You.

I sacrifice my opinions, perceptions, and desires to You. I want to exchange these for Your perspective. I give You permission to change my heart, and I choose to partner with You so that my mind is renewed. Thank You for being so generous with me.

Amen

Be encouraged! You are making progress and advancing. Your efforts to renew your mind are a great investment in your spirit and soul. The dividends are huge! Stay the course. We believe in you and are confident that, with His help, you can do this!

ACCOUNTABILITY

Connect with your accountability partner! Be open about what you're discovering. Transparency is good for spiritual growth and development. Their insight could be the instrument Holy Spirit wants to use to refine your thinking!

> "As iron sharpens iron, so a friend sharpens a friend."
> (Proverbs 27:17)

DAY 3

TODAY'S CHALLENGE :

Trash the autopilot.

STUDY

Let's talk about the words that originate from the thoughts in our hearts. It will take some time for new thinking to take hold and create a natural flow of positive words. For a bit, our mouths may get ahead of us, spewing out complaints. Until our thinking is renewed, we'll need to be just as intentional about our words as we are with our thoughts.

As we choose to *think* thoughts of love, joy, peace, hope, thankfulness, and praise, we'll also have to choose to *say* them. We will have to be deliberate in vocalizing love-filled, joyful, peaceful, hopeful thoughts. It's important to speak words of encouragement, support, and grace, and to declare our thankfulness and praise even if no one is there to hear it. We must let these new thoughts become the new words we say.

Let's be real about it—it might seem awkward at first. It might even sound corny to let those words roll off your tongue if you're not accustomed to speaking this way. You might even have a sense of embarrassment. Family and friends who aren't used to hearing you sound so positive and encouraging may wonder what's gotten into you or offer quizzical looks. They may even be offended because you are no longer speaking the same sarcastic or critical language they do.

But don't let it bother you. And don't get discouraged. Muscle through it, because those words are sweeter than you think to your own lips and to the ears of those who hear them. In time, those will be the words that easily flow from your heart and through your mouth without a second thought.

It's important to take action and speak these new words of gratitude and affirmation for several reasons. First, it's imperative because the spoken word has the power to create! If you'll remember, in chapter 1 we said:

> If we could see into the spirit realm, we'd see that every word we say has a creative force behind it that creates pathways for our future. Our intangible words are building something very tangible. Something concrete. They either create pathways of longevity, peace, blessing, and life, or they are building roads that lead to entrapment, chaos, ruin, and death.

We want to start speaking words full of truth as soon as possible to build pathways of life that lead to peace, blessing, and longevity.

Second, it's important to say them out loud because our lives will be filled with the fruit of our lips. Remember Proverbs 18:20–21 (AMP) says, "A man's stomach will be satisfied with the fruit of his mouth; He will be satisfied with the consequence of his words. Death and life are in the power of the tongue, And those who love it and indulge it will eat its fruit and bear the consequences of their words." Proverbs 12:14 (AMP) says, "A man will be satisfied with good from the fruit of his words." We want to speak—out loud—good words that crowd out the fruit of death and fill until we are bursting with the fruit of life!

Finally, we want to rewire our brains so that truth becomes our default, autopilot setting. We want to say truthful, love-filled, honoring words that create new neural pathways that enable us to associate truth with every circumstance. Truth-filled words are key in tearing down those strongholds in our minds!

It's a lot of work. This will not be easy and will not come naturally at first. But, speaking these words out loud is so profitable that it's worth any uncomfortableness we may feel!

Don't get discouraged if your mouth gets ahead of you. This is a process. It takes time to sever negative neural pathways and establish new pathways of truth. When you become aware of the old habit leaping from your lips, stop and regroup, even if you have to do it midsentence. Take the thoughts captive that fueled those words, surrender them to Jesus, and ask Him to exchange them for His perspective. Then, start again.

Today's challenge is awareness. Stop operating on autopilot and be fully cognizant of what you are saying and the tone in which you are saying it. The more aware you become, the more you'll grow into change.

Ask Holy Spirit to help you become aware of the words that are coming out of your mouth. Ask Him to show you the moment you go on autopilot. Give Him permission to draw your attention when your mouth gets ahead of you and to give you the strength to stop immediately and course correct. Ask Him to give you the power to change your words to ones that are full of life.

Did you realize you had an autopilot? What does being on autopilot look like for you?

_____

_____

_____

_____

How comfortable are you in saying words that are full of life? Even to strangers or people you are frustrated with?

_____

_____

_____

_____

ACTIVATION

Spend some time ruminating on these verses. Turn them over in your mind, looking at them from every angle, and then rest in them. Repeat the process until you've squeezed every ounce of truth from it! Rumination can't be hurried, so don't rush through. Take your time to listen for what Holy Spirit is saying to you.

READ

James 1:26, Proverbs 13:3, Proverbs 16:24, Psalm 141:3, Ephesians 4:29, Colossians 4:6, and Titus 3:1–2. Journal the insight you gain as He reveals truth from each verse.

ANSWER

1. Have you ever given much thought to your words before this Challenge? Why or why not?

   _____

   _____

   _____

   _____

   _____

2. What do you think you have created or built in your life with your words? As a result of your words, what is your life full of?

   _____

   _____

   _____

   _____

   _____

3. How does it feel to speak words that are positive, honoring, and encouraging when you want to complain, criticize, or argue?

    _____

    _____

    _____

4. Change will be a process. It will take time—lots of it—to completely rewire your brain and establish new thought patterns. How will you take advantage of this time? What can you do to make the most of this journey?

    _____

    _____

    _____

Memorize Psalm 19:14: "May the words of my mouth and the meditation of my heart be pleasing to you, O Lord, my rock and my redeemer."

Make it a good day by speaking life, and start by roaring your declaration statement!

REFLECTION

It's the end of Day 3. Selah! Time to breathe, pause, and reflect on the day. Contemplation is a necessary habit for facilitating change. It allows time and space for Holy Spirit to speak to our hearts and reveal things that we might otherwise miss. As you are looking back on the past 24 hours, here are a few things to consider:

What differences are you beginning to notice in your thinking?

_____

_____

_____

_____

What shifts have taken place in your perception or overall outlook? Your point of view on certain people? Situations?

_____

_____

_____

_____

Is it a bit easier to identify grumbling, complaining, and criticism? Is it becoming more obvious to you?

_____

_____

_____

What differences are you noticing in your words? Are there less complaints and criticisms flowing out?

_____

_____

_____

Prayer

Abba Father,

I confess to You that I have been a complainer and criticizer. I have been quick to engage in arguments. I repent of a lifetime of complaining. Help me become acutely aware of my words so that I have the opportunity to change them. Empower me to choose words that are full of thankfulness, honor, and love. I give You permission to reveal every aspect of complaining and criticism in my life and convict me when I choose critical or complaining words. Give me strength to live in the victory You've already given me.

And thank You for being so patient with me.

Amen

As you close out the day, take a moment to celebrate your victories! You are doing a great job of listening to Holy Spirit and receiving His corrections and instruction. You are becoming more attuned to His voice and growing in obedience. We are proud of you and the great strides you are making into deeper freedom!

ACCOUNTABILITY

Remember to connect with your accountability partner! Be straightforward with them on what you're experiencing. Don't brush over the struggle, the weight of conviction, or the difficulties you're having. Remember, there is a fine line between venting and processing. There is nothing wrong with acknowledging what you are experiencing. We encourage you to honestly share what you're going through, but do so without grumbling about how the Challenge is stretching you. We want you to be real with them because you need their encouragement and support. You'll never get anywhere if you're not truthful about how you feel.

"Just as iron sharpens iron, a person sharpens the character of his friend."
(Proverbs 27:17 CJB)

DAY 4

TODAY'S CHALLENGE :

Inspect your thoughts, attitudes, and words for opinions.

STUDY

By now we're sure you've realized just how much you complain and criticize. You've probably also discovered just how opinionated you are. If you're like us, nothing seems to be off limits and you have an opinion on most everything. If you're like Kim, you may even have *several* opinions about one thing.

At first glance this seems perfectly normal. We are surrounded by opinions. We live in a culture that celebrates opinions, encouraging everyone to have one about everything. We even solicit opinions. Pollsters want to know our thoughts on politics, shopping preferences, and everything in between. This has given us the impression that our opinions are more valuable and important than they really are.

Having an overinflated value of our opinions leads us into arguments. The root of every argument is a differing opinion. Arguments are nothing more than heated conversations where we insist that the way we see something is the right way. The *only* way. It's virtually impossible for our culture to amicably "agree to disagree" because we value our opinions so greatly.

This is also evidence that our self-worth is tied up in our opinions. We need everyone (or at least the majority) to agree with us so that we feel validated, accepted, and approved.

If you don't want my opinions or if you disagree me, I am angered, offended, and insulted because I feel devalued.

However, we are no longer of this world and don't live by society's standards. According to Philippians 3:20, "we are citizens of heaven." We live in the Kingdom of God, where being opinionated is not encouraged. You never find Jesus encouraging us to develop our own opinions. You never hear God instructing us to form ideas and thoughts based upon our perspective.

As we stated in chapter 2, not all opinions are bad. There's nothing wrong with believing jazz is better than country, peonies are prettier than roses, or U of M is superior to State. There's nothing wrong with having preferences or being partial to certain things. Our hardwiring and experiences contribute to our likes, dislikes, and proclivities to certain things. And, it makes life so much more interesting as the thoughts and ideas of others opens up new possibilities for us. Diversity allows us to see what we may otherwise miss.

But the reality is, we don't need an opinion about everything. We don't need to form opinions outside things that personally affect us. In other words, I don't need to have opinions about you or your life, like how you raise your children or spend your money. I don't need to have opinions about random things that don't concern me, like why you have so many bumper stickers on your car. I don't need opinions on how things are done in places over which I have no control, like how they organized the event.

The problem with opinions is that they are usually the soil where criticism blooms. They open the door for judgement. We're not talking issues of right and wrong. Scripture makes it clear that we should always present the truth boldly, but in *love*. What we're talking about is opinions on every day, common differences. Differences that have no eternal value. The differences that set us off, keep us frustrated, and start arguments.

We need to understand different is not necessarily wrong—it's just different. And when we value our opinion more than we value people, then we have an opinion problem.

In God's Kingdom, love and honor are valued above opinions. People are the treasure of the Kingdom. People are who Jesus came and died for. Abba Father values humanity above all creation. If our opinions inhibit us from loving others, then we are wrong. We believe Jesus sums this topic up in Matthew 22:39 when He said, "Love your neighbor as you love yourself." People come first, before what you think about any given subject.

The truth is, we should relinquish our opinions to Jesus and embrace His perspective on everything. Our opinions are clouded with human reasoning and near-sightedness, and sadly, our opinions are usually based upon selfishness instead of biblical truth. Only Jesus can see everything from every angle. Only He knows the hearts and motives of every person. His perspective is the only one that is complete, perfect, and true. In our opinions we are flying blind; with His perspective, we see clearly.

We challenge you today to inspect your thoughts and conversations for opinions. Ask Holy Spirit to draw your attention to unnecessary opinions. Ask Him to reveal to you any opinions that open the door for complaining, criticism, or arguing. Give Him permission to convict you. Once you see your opinions, surrender them and ask Him to replace them with His perspective.

What is the connection between opinions and arguments?

_____

_____

_____

_____

_____

How do differences of opinion cause you to be critical of people?

_____

_____

_____

_____

_____

ACTIVATION

Take some time to soak your heart in these Scriptures. Soaking your heart in the Word is like soaking in Epsom salt. Soaking in Epsom salt is said to prevent hardening of the arteries and removes toxins. That's exactly the benefits of soaking your heart in truth. It prevents hardening of the heart and it removes toxins from your spirit and soul.

READ

Luke 11:35 (TPT), Galatians 5:14–21 (TPT), Romans 12:10 (AMP) and Philippians 2:3 (TPT). Journal everything Holy Spirit reveals to you as you read each verse.

ANSWER

1. Were you surprised to discover how opinionated you are? Did you realize you have so many opinions about so many things?

   _____

   _____

   _____

   _____

2. Have you ever considered that some opinions could be a sin? Why or why not?

   _____

   _____

   _____

3. How should being a citizen of the Kingdom of God influence your opinions? How should it determine what opinions you should and should not have?

   _____

   _____

   _____

4. What toxic opinions has Holy Spirit revealed to you? What made them toxic to you?

_____

_____

_____

_____

You're gaining momentum, so don't stop now. Go out and make it a complaint-free day!

REFLECTION

It's the end of Day 4, which means it's introspection time. The time of day we look deep within to discover what's been hiding in plain sight. We think today may be a hard one for you because dealing with opinions is tough. However painful it may be, it's both healing and freeing. It's only when we are honest with ourselves that we can begin to deal with our issues head-on. The good news is Jesus is always with you to comfort you as you mourn over your sin. Lean into Him and draw strength for each stage of journey.

How have your opinions altered your perspective of the people and circumstances in your life?

_____

_____

_____

How have your opinions prevented you from seeing the whole picture? Seeing another's perspective? Caused you to devalue others?

_____

_____

_____

Do you think you'll be able to fully surrender your opinions to Jesus and submit to His perspective instead? Why or why not?

_____

_____

_____

Ask Holy Spirit to show you where you have developed unnecessary opinions and why you have a tendency to do that.

_____

_____

_____

Prayer

Abba Father,

I confess to You that I have been opinionated. I have unnecessarily formed opinions about people and situations, and I have allowed them to influence my words with complaints, criticism, or arguments. Forgive me for being opinionated. I choose to surrender my opinions and lay them at Your feet, Jesus. In exchange, will You give me Your perspective? Will You open my ears to hear what You hear and my eyes to see what You see? Will You let me feel with Your heart so deeply that it forms my opinions? Holy Spirit, I need Your help to live this way. Thank You for the grace You pour into my life.

Amen

As you wrap up the day, stop to appreciate how far you've come! In just four days you have made tremendous strides and covered a lot of ground. This is no small undertaking—you're changing your life! We applaud your courage and tenacity. Keep up the good work!

ACCOUNTABILITY

Make connection with your accountability partner. We know you're busy. We know you feel like you can handle this without them. We know you don't want to impose or inconvenience them. But you need this! You need the accountability. You need someone who will hold your feet to the fire and ask you the tough questions. So, call them. Spend some time being real. Talk with them about the impact your declaration statement is having on you. You'll thank us later.

> "You use steel to sharpen steel, and one friend sharpens another."
> (Proverbs 27:17 MSG)

DAY 5

TODAY'S CHALLENGE:

Inspect for self-criticism.

STUDY

Self-talk has been defined as our inner voice, or the ongoing dialogue in our head that runs constantly throughout the day and sometimes into the night. We are often the noise that keeps ourselves awake, as perpetual conversations play in our minds. While this persistent chatter can pertain to anything, we suspect a lot of it has to do with self-criticism.

It's important to know where self-criticism comes from. Self-criticism is not a helpful tool for personal growth. It is a destructive tool of the enemy. In John 10:10, Jesus gave us the inside scoop when He said, "The thief's purpose is to steal and kill and destroy. My purpose is to give them a rich and satisfying life." The number one mission of the enemy is to steal from us, kill things in our lives, and destroy us. And if he can get us to partner with him by turning the knife on ourselves, then it makes the job all the more pleasurable for him.

You may be thinking that defining self-criticism as a destructive tool of the enemy is a bit harsh and aggressive, but Revelation 12:10 clearly identifies our enemy as the relentless accuser of God's people who stands before God criticizing us night and day. When we criticize ourselves, we are partnering with the enemy, poisoning our own hearts with his lies.

146

We know they are lies because Jesus tells us in John 8:44 that the enemy is a liar and the father of lies. Everything he says is a lie. Every criticism he speaks about you is a lie. There is *nothing* true—no truth—in *anything* he says. One of the main keys to breaking free of criticism and rewiring your brain is to sever your partnership with the enemy and to refuse to speak his language any longer.

So, what should our self-talk sound like? It should mimic the words Jesus says about us verbatim. To know what He is saying about us, we first need to understand how Jesus feels about us. Despite what you may think, He is not annoyed, frustrated, disappointed, irritated, or disgusted with us. His thoughts about you are not ones of aggravation or displeasure. Instead, He cherishes you with every thought. He has more thoughts about you than there are grains of sand on every beach (Psalm 139:17–18). Take about ten minutes to let the reality of that sink in. Think of all the grains of sand on any beach you've been to. Then imagine all the beaches across the world. Imagine every single grain is a thought that cherishes—treasures, values, prizes, loves, and adores—you!

Every one of His thoughts about you is one of love, devotion, pleasure, affection, and warmth. His heart is not hard toward you. He is open to you, soft-hearted toward you. He adores you.

Even when you sin, He is not angry or disappointed. He lovingly grieves your disconnection from Him, and in love and faithfulness draws you home.

God is not tolerating you or putting up with you because He has to. He enjoys you. He finds pleasure in you. He joyfully, ecstatically, and enthusiastically sings over you with delight and gladness (Zephaniah 3:17). He rejoices over you and the wonder of who you are. He celebrates you—His amazing creation. It's not because you have done anything monumental. It is because you exist.

Even when your life is a chaotic mess, God finds pleasure in you because He sees in you all He created you to be. He sees the beauty—the gold—He wove into your being, and He longs to draw you into His arms, heal your brokenness, and unveil your beauty.

Today, we challenge you to focus the words you think and say to and about yourself—both internally and externally. Listen for your tone. Inspect your motive. Stop to realize where those words come from and what their intent is. Then, reject those words you know are from the enemy. Refuse to partner with words that were meant to steal, kill, and destroy you. In their place, choose the words Jesus says about you. If you don't know what He is saying about you, stop and ask Him what He thinks of you. Ask if He will let you hear the song He is singing over you right then. Then, begin to sing with Him, for you will never say anything truer about yourself than His words. His words fill you with abundant life. It's a beautiful way to rewire your brain.

How have you been using the tool of self-criticism?

_____

_____

_____

_____

_____

How does it make you feel to know that God is singing joyfully over you?

_____

_____

_____

_____

_____

ACTIVATION

Each day we've encouraged you to "take your time" and journey with Holy Spirit as you read the verses listed in this section. We do this because the Bible is a spiritual letter written by God, and you are reading it with human understanding. To us, this is like trying to read a letter written to you in a foreign language. While you may understand some of the letters used to form the words, grasping the meaning of those words is difficult . . . if not impossible. Never rush through reading the Bible as if you are checking an item off your to-do list. Always take your time and process the words with your translator, Holy Spirit. This ensures you get everything possible from each reading experience.

We know some of these verses may be very familiar to you. If so, we encourage you to read them in various translations to help you gain new insights and greater revelation.

READ

Psalm 18:19, Psalm 139:16–18, Zephaniah 3:17, Jeremiah 29:11, Romans 8:38–39, and Ephesians 2:10. Journal everything Holy Spirit interprets to you as you read each verse.

ANSWER

1. Did you realize that self-criticism is partnership with the enemy?

   _____

   _____

   _____

   _____

2. What are some lies you believe about yourself that cause you to be critical of yourself?

   _____

   _____

   _____

   _____

3. Why is it hard for you to believe what God says about you?

   _____

   _____

   _____

   _____

4. How do you think your life would change if you began to speak to yourself the way God speaks to you?

_____

_____

_____

_____

5. How do you plan to change your self-talk?

_____

_____

_____

_____

Enjoy your day as you agree with God and repeat to yourself what He is saying about you!

REFLECTION

As you take some time to soul search tonight, the end of Day 5, carefully look at how you treat yourself. Self-examination can be healthy, but it can also be destructive. The goal is not to overwhelm yourself with criticism. Your goal is to journey with Holy Spirit so He can tenderly show you specific issues that need your attention. He never intends for you to handle them yourself. His plan is to partner with you to give you everything you need to succeed. Self-examination with Holy Spirit leaves you with hope and promise.

Why do you think you speak critically to yourself?

_____

_____

_____

How has self-criticism hindered you spiritually? Emotionally? In relationships?

_____

_____

_____

What limitations has self-criticism placed on you?

_____

_____

_____

How will you prepare yourself to combat the lies the enemy hurls at you? What truth will you use to up root those lies?

_____

_____

_____

_____

Prayer

Abba Father,

I confess to You that I have been abusing myself with criticism.

Forgive me for partnering with the enemy and speaking words of death over myself.

Please open my eyes to see You rejoicing over me.

Please open my ears so that I can hear Your celebrations

and the songs You sing over me. Please show me how You feel about me.

I long to hear what You think of me so that I can begin to repeat those words to myself.

I choose to forgive myself for devaluing and damaging myself through words of criticism. I release myself from this debt and choose to love myself the same way Jesus loves me.

Amen

Take a moment to recount your successes. Look at all the times you took thoughts captive, were intentional with your words, allowed Holy Spirit to convict you, and exchanged your opinion for His perspective. Woohoo! We celebrate your success and are confident this is just the beginning of a brand-new life for you!

ACCOUNTABILITY

One of the most important people in your life is your accountability partner. Let them challenge you. Allow them space to probe and question your motives and reasoning. They can often see things that you're too close to see. They recognize issues you've normalized. They can help you hurdle roadblocks to your freedom. Prioritize this connection—you need them!

> "It takes a grinding wheel to sharpen a blade,
> and so one person sharpens the character of another."
> (Proverbs 27:17 TPT)

DAY 6

TODAY'S CHALLENGE :

Look for the gold in others.

STUDY

Yesterday we asked you to inspect for self-criticism, and we challenged you to exchange your harsh words about yourself for His life-giving words about you. We asked you to tackle this issue first because it's nearly impossible to stop criticizing others until you stop criticizing yourself.

Part of loving others is honoring them with your words. Jesus said it like this in Matthew 22:39, "Love your neighbor as yourself." How you treat others is directly connected to how your treat yourself.

So, who exactly is our neighbor? Anybody. Everybody. It's not just the person who lives next door to you or the guy in the cubicle next to you. It's any person on the planet. It's every person you encounter. It's the people you know *and* the people you don't know. The directive from Jesus in Matthew 22:39 is to love all of them the way you love yourself. So, if we are not supposed to criticize ourselves, then we are not supposed to criticize them either.

We won't even try to make this one seem easy. This is hard. Really hard. It's hard because, in our opinions (there's that risky word!), some people are just not loveable. From our point of view (see how it creeps in there!), some people are difficult to love. From our perspective (eek—so many disguises!), we can't love them because they are too different.

153

Too complicated. Too evil. Too messed up. Too mean. See why we need to get rid of our opinions?

To help us succeed in this difficult task, Jesus gives us a great way to learn to love our neighbor. In Matthew 7:12, He institutes the Golden Rule: "Do to others whatever you would like them to do to you." While we may be comfortable criticizing ourselves internally, we never appreciate or want criticism from an outside source. It cuts us, wounding deeply, leaving scars. Whether it is said directly to us or we hear about it through the grapevine, it feels demeaning, deflating, and embarrassing. This is never something we want done to us. So, it should never be something we do to another.

The Golden Rule takes us past the "don't" and propels us into the "do." Living the Golden Rule means we don't just refrain from doing harm, but we go the extra mile and treat people in the way we would like to be treated. Within the context of this book, we don't just withhold criticism, we go the extra mile and say good things. We choose to verbalize things that build others up and bless them. We choose to speak words that encourage and edify. We say *to* others what we'd want them to say *to* us. We say *about* others what we'd want them to say *about* us. We speak of them in the way we want to be spoken of—favorable and kindly.

Sometimes it can be difficult to find something good to say about people or circumstances. We are not suggesting that you exaggerate, lie, or be fake. We don't even think you should compliment a negative as if it were a positive. The best approach is to ask Holy Spirit to show you what the Father sees in that person or situation. Ask Him to let you see through His eyes and hear through His ears. Ask Him to allow you to feel with His heart. Then it will be much easier to see the gold in them and recognize their value. You'll have clarity about situations when you catch His heartbeat on it. From that vantage point, you'll want to acknowledge what He sees and hears.

This perspective is precisely how Jesus intends for His followers to live. It's the governing principle of the Kingdom meant to influence our thoughts, words, and actions. It's firm and unmovable. There are no exceptions. No exemption clauses. Nothing that allows us to live any other way.

With that in mind, today's challenge asks you to intentionally look for gold in the people and situations you encounter. When you are tempted to criticize anything—or even as you criticize anything—stop and ask Holy Spirit to show you the positive in them. This is a good time to proclaim your declaration statement. It will help you prepare for the day's challenge!

Why is it hard to believe that there is gold in every person?

_____

_____

_____

Do you feel fake when you search to find something to compliment instead of criticizing the obvious? Why or why not?

_____

_____

_____

ACTIVATION

Take your time and really dig into these verses. Be like an archeologist, excavating the treasures of antiquity. Carefully filter through layers to mine the wealth of truth contained within. Use Bible study tools to help you better understand what you're discovering. Ask Holy Spirit to be your magnifying glass, amplifying what you're discovering. Don't rush, or you'll miss details that are life changing!

READ

Galatians 5:14 (TPT), Romans 13:10 (TPT), James 4:11–12 (TPT), Luke 6:37–42 (TPT), and Proverbs 12:18. Journal everything Holy Spirit reveals to you as you read each verse.

ANSWER

1. Have you ever equated criticism with being judgmental? Now that you realize this, explain the connection.

   _____

   _____

   _____

   _____

2. Why do you find it difficult to say good things to or about certain people and situations?

   _____

   _____

   _____

   _____

3. What do you tend to be most critical about? Why do you think this particular area is one you struggle with?

   _____

   _____

   _____

   _____

4. List the top three people you have been most critical of.

   _____

   _____

   _____

   _____

5. Ask Holy Spirit to reveal the Father's heart for these people to you. Listen and then list at least one positive thing about each person.

_____

_____

_____

_____

6. How would it change your life if you had the Father's perspective on every person and situation you encounter?

_____

_____

_____

_____

Approach today like a treasure hunt, searching for the gold in others. And remember to shout it out when you find it!

REFLECTION

At the end of this sixth day, remember that stretching is a great exercise for your physical body, because it increases blood flow, flexibility, and your range of motion. Reflection is stretching for the soul. When done in partnership with Jesus, it enables His blood to flow to every area of your life, enables you to grow in flexibility (so you are less rigid emotionally), and increases our range of motion, enabling us to do what we may not have been able to do otherwise.

Today as you spend time reflecting with Jesus, stretch yourself to look at areas that are painful. Together with Holy Spirit, inspect the critical places of your heart. Struggle to work out the kinks so that you can become more flexible and able to love all your neighbors. As you do, His blood will pump through your veins and repair those broken places.

How has self-criticism influenced your thoughts and feelings about others? How has this bred a judgmental attitude in you?

_____

_____

_____

_____

_____

How does being critical make you feel? Empowered? Better? Weaker? Ashamed? Smarter?

_____

_____

_____

_____

Why do you think being critical makes you feel this way?

_____

_____

_____

_____

What do you think life would be like if you never criticized another person or situation again? How do you think it would change your relationships? How would it change your attitude and expectations? How would it change your experiences?

_____

_____

_____

How do you plan to stop critical and judgmental thoughts, so you can stop critical words?

_____

_____

_____

_____

_____

Prayer

Abba Father,

I confess to You that I have been critical and judgmental. I repent for forming my own opinions on people and situations instead of seeking Your heart on the matter. Holy Spirit, I give You permission to convict me every time I revert to critical and judgmental thinking. Fill me with Your perspective on everything and empower me to choose words that honor others. Thank You for forgiveness and being patient with me.

Amen

We hope you see how great you're doing! We know it might be hard to see how much progress you're making right now but trust us—you are! It's like watching grass grow. It seems as if nothing is happening, but deep inside growth is taking place. Keep at it, and it won't be long before you (and others) are able to see changes in you!

ACCOUNTABILITY

Check in with your accountability partner. Take time to discuss struggles, and devise a game plan for implementing change. Be detailed on how you are going to improve, but discussing your victories is equally important. Celebrate and inspect them together. Look at how you moved from the struggle into the victory. Note the pivotal moments and talk about how you can implement that strategy in other areas. It's worth the work!

> "As iron sharpens iron, So one man sharpens [and influences]
> another [through discussion]."
> (Proverbs 27:17 AMP)

DAY 7

TODAY'S CHALLENGE :

Practice thankfulness.

STUDY

The goal of this book is to help you shift from a complaining and critical mind-set to one that is honoring, encouraging, and peaceful. We think one of the best exercises you can do to help you make this transition is to practice thankfulness. The more thankful you are, the less likely you are to complain, criticize, and argue.

We know there are times when it's difficult to find something to be thankful for, but there is always *something*. Intentionally look for things to be thankful for. Talk about thankfulness. When thankfulness is brought to your attention, you begin to notice even more things you can be thankful for. Soon, you'll start to notice them everywhere.

It's a phenomenon called "frequency illusion." In very simple terms, it's the ability to notice things that have been all around you, but you did not recognize them until you were prompted to see them. In other words, you find what you are looking for.

So how do we prompt ourselves to notice things we can be thankful for? First, ask Holy Spirit to open your eyes to all the good things that surround you. Ask Him to show you His hand at work in your life. Ask Him to expose all the benefits and blessings He's pouring into your life. They are there; you just need to see them.

As you see them, stop and focus on them. Stare at the goodness He reveals to you. Fixate on the blessings. Fill your heart and mind with the good things He's exposing to you. This is crucial for the next step. Matthew 12:34 says, "For whatever is in your heart determines what you say." Some translations express it like this: "out of the abundance of the heart" (ESV, KJV, NKJV). Your words come from what's overflowing in your heart. Complaining, critical, and argumentative words reveal an excess of negativity, judgment, and hostility—and they have no place in the life of a follower of Jesus. If you are going to change your words, you need to stuff your heart and mind full of God's goodness so that the overflow is thankfulness, gratitude, and appreciation.

Next, exercise those thoughts. Talk about what He's showing you. Talk about the blessings. Talk about His goodness to you. Talk about what He's done. Talk about what He's doing. Talk about what Holy Spirit is revealing to you. No matter how big or how small, talk about it to everyone everywhere because those reps are building solid mental muscle, packing your soul with the weight of truth in your heart. And it's going a long way to rewire your brain!

While you're at it, crank out some reps on thankfulness. Talk about how important gratitude is. Talk about the benefits of being grateful. Talk about the spiritual significance of being thankful. Talk about the impact thankfulness has on your thinking and emotions. Have conversations with your accountability partner about it. Talk to your co-workers about it. Discuss it at the dinner table with your family. Ask them how they feel about it. The more you talk about something, the more aware you become of it.

Then, practice thankfulness. There are so many ways you can do this. We'll share a few ideas with you, but once you start practicing, we're sure you can think of more ways to incorporate thankfulness into your life!

- Daily journal something you are thankful for, no matter how insignificant it may seem.

- Make a gratitude jar and fill it with every good thing you experience. As an extra bonus, write your notes on colorful paper!

- Once a month, pull out the notes from your gratitude jar and read them to yourself or your family. (This is a *great* way to teach your kids thankfulness!) When done, put them back into the jar so you can read them again, along with the new ones you are adding to it.

- Say thank you to everyone for even the smallest gestures. Say thank you for things you don't normally say thank you for, like your spouse preparing dinner, the waitress bringing you water, or your child doing their homework.

Finally, prepare yourself to be thankful. This requires your slowing down. We live life so fast, it's hard to notice good things unless they are explosive. Intentionally slow yourself down so you can see all the good things that surround you. Get plenty of rest. It's easier to be thankful when you're well rested because your mind is more clear and less cranky. And pray. Talking to God primes your heart for thankfulness because it syncs your heart with His.

Practicing this is particularly important in difficult times and stressful situations. There will be times it seems impossible to find anything to be thankful for. We know what that feels like. When we stepped into the Blight of '17, there seemed very little to be thankful for. We had to search for something. We started with: "Father, we thank You for exposing this problem so we could be removed from it."

It was a start. And as the situation unfolded, we continued to add:

"We are grateful for wisdom and urgency of the elders of The River, who helped us navigate our way through this problem. Thank You, Father, for providing a good place to stay while we transitioned. We appreciate the support of our River Family as they prayed for us and offered their help. We are so thankful that there are some possessions we are able to remediate and keep."

The more we practiced thankfulness, the more thankful we became. Being thankful shifted our focus and enabled us to successfully navigate the difficulties of our situation. Being thankful did not change our situation, but it did change us and how we journeyed through it.

Another benefit of practicing thankfulness is that you're rewiring your brain. Practicing thankfulness means you can more easily and efficiently articulate thankfulness and gratitude. Repeating appreciation reorganizes your brain to make future thankfulness more likely. When you speak words of gratitude, your brain is restructured to naturally find the things to be grateful for. It becomes easy to see the blessings and provisions of God in your circumstances. Thankfulness becomes your default behavior and your native language. This is continually reinforced as you continue to express appreciation for all the good you see.

So today, we challenge you to make a plan to become more thankful. Write it down. Be specific on what you need to do. Get supplies. Inform your accountability partner. Talk to Jesus about this and ask Holy Spirit to empower you. Then implement it. Be intentional on practicing thankfulness because your success depends on it.

How does the pace of your life affect your ability to recognize the goodness of God in your life?

_____

_____

_____

_____

How often do you talk about the blessings of God in your life? Is it more, equal to, or less than your conversations containing complaints?

_____

_____

_____

_____

ACTIVATION

When you launch a boat, you are setting it in motion to do what it was created to do: sail. Activation is a lot like launching a boat; you're putting truth into operation so that you can do what you were created to do. Take your time and prepare for a successful launch so you can sail through life full of thankfulness and gratitude.

READ

1 Thessalonians 5:16–18, Ephesians 5:20, Colossians 3:15, Colossians 4:2, and Psalm 69:30. Journal everything Holy Spirit reveals to you as you read each verse.

ANSWER

1. Why do you think living in thankfulness is difficult for you?

   _____

   _____

   _____

   _____

   _____

2. What do you think about these two statements: God inhabits the praises of His people, not their complaints. Complaints actually glorify the enemy.

   _____

   _____

   _____

   _____

   _____

3. Name the most thankful people you know. How do you feel when you spend time with them? What do you think contributes to their thankfulness? Interview them about this topic.

_____

_____

_____

_____

4. In what ways will being thankful improve your life? How will gratefulness change your attitude?

_____

_____

_____

_____

5. In what ways does thankfulness draw you closer to God?

_____

_____

_____

_____

It's time to hit the ground running. And remember, no matter what happens, be thankful all day!

REFLECTION

Here at the end of Day 7, let's think about how much learning takes place when we implement change. We're activating new behavior, engaging different parts of our brain, and discovering new possibilities as we rewire our brain. With so much internal activity taking place, it's important to stop and reflect. This gives our brains the space needed to connect all the dots. It allows you to gain additional insight and connect with your feelings about everything that is going on inside you. Take your time as you think through these questions and tie them together with all you're experiencing.

How has ingratitude created problems in your life?

_____

_____

_____

_____

_____

_____

What do you think the roots of ingratitude are?

_____

_____

_____

_____

_____

_____

Which root is in your life?

_____

_____

_____

_____

_____

_____

How does the fact that ingratitude is a sin make you feel?

_____

_____

_____

_____

_____

Prayer

Abba Father,

I confess I have been ungrateful. Forgive me for not being aware of Your goodness in my life and all the blessings You have given me. Forgive me for complaining instead of purposing to find something to be thankful for.

Help me to see Your hand in my life. Open my eyes to Your blessings in my life and help me to see Your fingerprints in everything. Holy Spirit, empower me to express thanksgiving every day regardless of what I see or feel. Thank You for all the good things You've given me. I appreciate You and am grateful for all You've done.

Amen

As you close out this Challenge, take note of all the changes that have taken place in you since you started this journey. Acknowledge your struggles and appreciate the pain of each. Note the revelations you received and the breakthroughs they brought. You have covered a lot of ground during this experience and you will never be the same. That is worth celebrating! Father God is so proud of you and is singing songs of deliverance over you. We applaud you and are so excited for all the benefits you will reap as a result of your hard work. We continue to pray for you as you continue on this journey into the heart of freedom.

ACCOUNTABILITY

By now you know we think connection with your accountability partner is crucial! Just because your journey is over doesn't mean you need to stop this valuable relationship. It's been instrumental in your success and it will continue to be an important part of your journey. Make the time. Plan for it. Work it into your schedule. Do whatever it takes to maintain this relationship. They keep you sharp and ready for battle!

> "You use steel to sharpen steel, and one friend sharpens another."
> (Proverbs 27:17 MSG)

CONCLUSION

THAT'S A WRAP!

It's over. You made it! You survived the Challenge and lived to tell the tale. You are a success!

Let's look back over our time in the Challenge and meditate on how far we've come.

What changes do you notice in your thinking?

_____

_____

_____

_____

_____

How has your perception and overall outlook shifted?

_____

_____

_____

_____

_____

CONCLUSION

How has your point of view changed on certain people or situations?

_____

_____

_____

_____

_____

How quickly do you notice your complaining, critical, and argumentative thoughts?

_____

_____

_____

_____

_____

Can you tell a difference in your words? Are there fewer complaints and criticisms flowing out? Is there more thankfulness and compliments flowing out?

_____

_____

_____

_____

_____

Recount a time when you stopped yourself and changed your words midstream?

_____

_____

_____

_____

_____

How are your relationships different?

_____

_____

_____

_____

_____

How has the atmosphere of your home or work changed?

_____

_____

_____

_____

_____

Who has noticed a change in you? What did they say?

_____

_____

_____

_____

_____

How do you feel?

_____

_____

_____

_____

_____

How has your self-talk changed?

_____

_____

_____

_____

_____

What areas do you still need to work on?

_____

_____

_____

_____

_____

What is your plan to walk in this change?

_____

_____

_____

_____

_____

You have done so well and accomplished so much. Your hard work and relentless efforts are paying off as you have made great headway in removing complaining from your life. But if you're like us, you're not done. We encourage you to keep going.

We know this is not easy. We felt the same challenges and difficulties you felt. We grew tired of relentlessly inspecting thoughts and surrendering words. It was exhausting mentally and emotionally. At times it still is, as we continue to root out this issue from our lives. But we believe the difference it makes is worth the investment. It's worth the struggle. The reward is so much greater than the sacrifice.

Cognitive neuroscientist Dr. Caroline Leaf says that it can take anywhere from three to four 21-day cycles to establish new, healthy thought patterns.[15] You are seven days in. Seven days closer. Take this momentum and keep going. Keep journaling. Keep looking at these verses. Keep asking yourself the Reflection questions. Talk about it with your spouse and kids. Talk about it with co-workers. Make it a regular part of your conversations so that it stays in the forefront of your mind.

We strongly encourage you to memorize the Scriptures we list in the Challenge and throughout the book. It's not just for kids in Sunday school. Memorization is a powerful tool for rewiring our brains. Remember the concepts of neuroplasticity and the malleable brain. You can change your auto-pilot responses. Imagine the possibilities if you rewired your brain so truth automatically shaped your thoughts and flowed from your mouth. How different would your life be? That can be your reality, if you'll include Scripture memorization in your journey into freedom.

Psalm 119:11 (AMP) encourages us to do just that: "Your word I have treasured and stored in my heart, That I may not sin against You." When you memorize Scripture, you are training your brain to turn to truth first. Truth becomes your default setting and is the first thing to rise to the surface in any situation. When you use the explosive power of truth, you'll see strongholds tumble much more quickly. So, be intentional to memorize the Word.

Post these verses on sticky notes or index cards on your bathroom mirror, tape them to your steering wheel, fix them to the fridge, make them your screensaver on your computer and phone. Put them where your eyes scan throughout the day, and be intentional to actually look at them, say them out loud, and commit them to memory.

Keep proclaiming your declaration statement. Make it a part of your daily routine. As you grow and develop in this area, you may want to edit or change. We believe that once you discover how powerful it is, your declaration will grow and expand! You may even write more for other areas of your life. Be sure to write them full of Scripture so they will be powerful and effective!

CONCLUSION

Stay with your accountability partner. Keep having honest and authentic discussions with them. Be open about your setbacks and struggles. Celebrate your successes with them. Let them encourage you to stay on track and reach your goal.

Read the first eleven chapters again. Do the pre-challenge workouts again. Do them often. They are great barometers for measuring progress. Do the Challenge again. And again. Do it as many times as it takes to get free from complaining and criticism. Nothing these sins offer you can compare to the delight that freedom brings you. Nothing.

One last suggestion: read the book of Proverbs. It's thirty-one chapters; read one chapter a day. It's full of good stuff. Dig into the verses about the mouth, tongue, and words. Don't just glaze over them. Read them as if you've never seen them before. Ask Holy Spirit to open your mind and give you clarity and understanding before you read. Journal what He shows you. These will give you a solid study for thirty-ones days and will help you as you continue with this Challenge!

We'll leave you with a few more Scriptures to absorb. They will be a great encouragement as you continue the journey. Take some time now to read Psalm 119:57–60, John 14:26, Philippians 1:6, and Galatians 6:7–9.

EPILOGUE

In the time since we moved out after discovering toxic levels of mold and formaldehyde in the parsonage, God has done amazing things. He has taken such good care us, and no detail has been left undone.

First, He provided the perfect house for us. While I (Kim) thought we needed the house we originally made an offer on, God knew the one we really needed and guided us directly to it—the very next day. We were the first and only people to see it. The For Sale sign never made it into the lawn. We stepped in and immediately knew this was His provision for us. It was move-in ready, painted in wonderful colors, and came with all the appliances, which is a big deal when you have none. As testimony to how thoroughly He covers every detail, the sellers were also selling most of their furniture. It was in great shape (some virtually new) and we liked it! You won't believe what a huge blessing this was for us. He took care of everything. No detail was left undone. We can't tell you how much we appreciate this gift. Every day we walk through our home and thank Him for being so generous to us.

Our recovery has progressed nicely. When we discovered the mold and formaldehyde issue, we were both prescribed dozens of medications. In addition to that, I (Bill) had countless tests done by several doctors and specialists: MRI, ultrasound, X-rays, heart tests, balance and equilibrium testing, a sleep study, countless blood draws, multiple visits to the ER, endless appointments with our regular doctors, several visits with a homeopathic doctor, visits to an ENT, a neurologist, and more. Kim had allergy testing, CT scans, and many blood draws with several doctors. Now, Kim no longer takes any medication, and I only take one thyroid medication. We count that as a great success. To say we are in a much better place is an understatement. Our doctor appointments have tapered off greatly and Jesus connected us with a great naturopathic doctor who loves Him and prayed for us as she treated us. This was another great blessing!

While I (Bill) am still experiencing some issues and have not returned to my "normal" self, I am better and remain confident that God will continue to heal my body and resolve these lingering issues. I believe I will finish in better health than I was before this crisis started.

The changes we made to our diet and lifestyle helped our bodies expedite recovery and has enhanced our quality of life. This is one of the reasons we are so thankful for the Blight of '17. We would never have taken such drastic measures to improve our health if we had not been forced to. The results of the Blight are that we're much heathier now. And once I (Kim) chose to be thankful for the food changes and embraced healthy eating, it made things a lot easier, much to Bill's relief. The day I cried all through dinner was a little stressful for him. While I still don't like broccoli, I am learning to live without sugar, and appreciate honey and agave!

Our greatest blessing of all has been the Challenge itself. Engaging in conversation and participating in challenges prior to the Blight not only positioned us for success as we navigated through it, but also has changed the trajectory of our lives. It gave us new lenses that enable us to see things more clearly, to see things from His perspective.

While we still have our moments where we find complaining or critical thoughts rising to the surface and sometimes easing their way out of our mouths, we are so much more aware now. And awareness is half the battle! We are equipped to arrest them, take them captive, and exchange them for His thoughts and words. The Challenge has changed the way we feel about people and situations. It has made Jesus's command to love more natural. It's changed our thoughts on everything from the weather to traffic to unexpected inconveniences. It has changed the way we think about ourselves. It changes how we see others.

We also have so much more joy! Before the Blight of '17 we were confident in God. We knew His character and were intimate with His nature. However, after going through this experience, this has deepened exponentially. The more we learn and the deeper we go, we realize we are only scratching the surface! He is so much more than we ever imagined, and this causes our confidence to soar. And with that come deeper peace and abounding hope. We feel lighter. Freer. And it was worth every tear, every sigh, every painful and disappointing moment. It was worth all the loss. It was worth the struggle. We would not change this experience for the world.

We can truly say that what the enemy intended to crush us with, God has used to bless and enrich our lives. He has worked all this together for our good, and He's not finished yet. We are certain that the best is yet to come!

Thank you for purchasing this book and joining us for the Challenge. Thank you for letting us be with you for part of your journey. We are honored that you would allow us to partner with you in this way. We hope the Challenge has been as life changing for you as it has been for us. We pray the fruit of your efforts continue to unfold in your life and you experience all Jesus has for you!

NOTES

1. Zig Ziglar, *Ziglar on Selling: The Ultimate Handbook for the Complete Sales Professional* (Nashville: Thomas Nelson, 1991), 163.

2. If you'd like to read more about the impact of your words, we highly recommend *The Power of Your Words* by Robert Morris.

3. Ainslie Johnstone, "The amazing phenomenon of muscle memory," *Medium*, December 14, 2017, https://medium.com/oxford-university/the-amazing-phenomenon-of-muscle-memory-fb1cc4c4726.

4. If you'd like to read more about neuroplasticity and the malleable brain, we recommend reading *Who Switched Off My Brain?* and *Switch On Your Brain* by cognitive neuroscientist Dr. Caroline Leaf.

5 A Vulcan is a fictional, extraterrestrial character from Star Trek. They are distinguished by their lack of emotion and live solely by logic and reasoning. In the series, Mr. Spock is the main Vulcan character.

6. Evan Andrews, "Patrick Henry's 'Liberty or Death' Speech," History.com, March 22, 2015, https://www.history.com/news/patrick-henrys-liberty-or-death-speech-240-years-ago.

7. *Bambi,* directed by James Alger et al, (1942; Walt Disney Productions).

8. Udanavarga 518 Baha'u'llah Gleanings

9. Mahabharata 5:1517

10. Baha'u'llah Gleanings

11. Reader, rest assured that this isn't a typo. We refuse to dignify the enemy enough to capitalize his name because he doesn't deserve it.

12. George Santayana, *Reason in Common Sense: The Life of Reason: The Phases of Human Progress* (Auckland, New Zealand: The Floating Press, 2009), 312.

13. Note: Neither polygamy nor bigamy were ever a part of God's plan. Ever. He neither sanctioned nor ordained this type of marriage. This is obvious when you look at each polygamist or bigamist marriage in Scripture. There was always strife and conflict. None of them fared well. Both polygamy and bigamy existed because God granted humanity the ability to choose (free will), and we often do foolish things with our choices.

14. 1 Corinthians 13, Ephesians 4:32, 1 Corinthians 1:10, and Philippians 2:4 are woven into this declaration.

15. Dr. Caroline Leaf, *Switch On Your Brain* (Grand Rapids: Baker Books, 2013), 153–154.

ABOUT THE AUTHORS

Bill and Kim Wahl serve as lead pastors at The River Church, a vibrant multicultural, multiethnic, multigenerational church in Fort Gratiot, Michigan. They are passionate proponents of discipleship who desire to see Heaven manifested in the lives of believers. Both are high-impact teachers who love to share biblical truths that help people change the way they think and react to the world around them. Bill and Kim have been married for more than thirty years and have three amazing children, two wonderful sons-in-law, and two adorable grandchildren.